VIEWPOINTS ON
MODERN WORLD HISTORY

Peace in the Middle East

Other Books of Related Interest

At Issue Series

Can the War on Terrorism Be Won?
Is Iran a Threat to Global Security?
What Role Should the U.S. Play in the Middle East?

Current Controversies Series

The Middle East
Politics and Religion

Opposing Viewpoints Series

Extremism
Iran
Islamic Militancy
Israel

VIEWPOINTS ON
MODERN WORLD HISTORY

Peace in the Middle East

Marty Gitlin, Book Editor

GREENHAVEN
PUBLISHING

Published in 2018 by Greenhaven Publishing, LLC
353 3rd Avenue, Suite 255, New York, NY 10010

First Edition

Articles in Greenhaven Publishing anthologies are often edited for length to meet page
requirements. In addition, original titles of these works are changed to clearly present
the main thesis and to explicitly indicate the author's opinion. Every effort is made to
ensure that Greenhaven Publishing accurately reflects the original intent of the authors.
Every effort has been made to trace the owners of the copyrighted material.

Cover image: Cynthia Johnson/The LIFE Images Collection/Getty Images

Library of Congress Cataloging-in-Publication Data

Names: Gitlin, Martin, editor.
Title: Peace in the Middle East / Martin Gitlin, book editor.
Description: First edition. | New York, NY : Greenhaven Publishing, 2018. |
  Series: Viewpoints on Modern World History | Audience: Grades 9-12.
Identifiers: LCCN 2017023234 | ISBN 9781534501430 (library bound)
Subjects: LCSH: Arab-Israeli conflict--1993---Peace. | Middle East--Politics
  and government--20th century. | Middle East--Politics and government--21st
  century. | IS (Organization) | United States--Foreign relations--Middle
  East. | Middle East--Foreign relations--United States.
Classification: LCC DS119.76 .P399 2018 | DDC 956.04--dc23
LC record available at https://lccn.loc.gov/2017023234

Manufactured in the United States of America

Website: http://greenhavenpublishing.com

Contents

Chapter 1: A Historical Perspective

The narrative that the continued struggle for peace in the Middle East is about political power is a dangerous one. It remains mostly about religion.

Foreword

"The more we know about the past enables us to ask richer and more provocative questions about who we are today. We also must tell the next generation one of the great truths of history: that no past event was preordained. Every battle, every election, and revolution could have turned out differently at any point along the way, just as a person's own life can change unpredictably."

—David McCullough, American historian

History is punctuated by momentous events—turning points for the nations involved, with impacts felt far beyond their borders. Displaying the full range of human capabilities—from violence, greed, and ignorance to heroism, courage, and strength—they are nearly always complicated and multifaceted. Any student of history faces the challenge of grasping both the broader elements and the nuances of world-changing events, such as wars, social movements, and environmental disasters. Textbooks offer only so much help, burdened as they are by constraints of length and single-perspective narratives. True understanding of history's significant events comes from exposure to a variety of perspectives from the people involved intimately, as well as those observing from a distance of miles or years.

Viewpoints on Modern World History examines global events from the twentieth century onward, presenting analysis and observation from numerous vantage points. The series offers high school, early college level, and general interest readers a thematically arranged anthology of previously published materials that address a major historical event or period. Each volume opens with background information on the event, presents the controversies surrounding the event, and concludes with the implications and legacy of the event. By providing a variety of perspectives, this series can be used to inform debate, help develop critical thinking skills, increase global awareness, and enhance an understanding of international viewpoints on history.

Material in each volume is selected from a diverse range of sources. Articles taken from these sources are carefully edited and introduced to provide context and background.

Each volume in the Viewpoints on Modern World History series also includes:

- An annotated **table of contents** that provides a brief summary of each essay in the volume
- An **introduction** specific to the volume topic
- A **chapter preface** setting up the chapter content and providing historical context
- For each viewpoint, a brief **introduction** that has notes about the author and source of the viewpoint and provides a summary of its main points
- Informational **sidebars** that explore the lives of key individuals, give background on historical events, or explain scientific or technical concepts
- A **chronology** of dates important to the period
- A **bibliography** of additional books, periodicals, and websites for further research
- A **subject index** that offers links to people, places, and events cited in the text

Viewpoints on Modern World History is designed for a broad spectrum of readers who want to learn more about not only history but also current events, political science, government, international relations, and sociology. This includes students doing research for class assignments or debates, teachers and faculty seeking to supplement course materials, and others wanting to improve their understanding of history. The volumes in this series are designed to illuminate a complicated event, to spark debate, and to show the human perspective behind the world's most significant happenings of recent decades.

Introduction

*"What I'm suggesting is we are going to look back,
and we're going to see what happened in Syria, and
we're going to see the larger destabilization of the
Middle East, the rise of extremism, and we're going
to wonder... Why didn't we at least try to force a
political solution — at an acceptable cost to us,
because no one is saying we should send in ground
troops — and if we did it would be worse than doing
nothing... If we do not act, we are going to look back
and wonder why we didn't."*

> *– Anne-Marie Slaughter, president and CEO
> of the New America Foundation*

The Impossible Dream" from the Broadway musical *Man of
La Mancha* does not refer to any political stalemate in the
Middle East, but it seems that no three words better describe the
possibility of bringing long-lasting peace to this troubled region.

Many singular issues have played roles in promoting the hate
and violence and chaos that has plagued that area of the world for
generations. The staggering number and intensity of religious and
territorial disputes have shown no signs of dissipating. In fact, the
rise of terrorism has worsened the conflicts.

Though the Middle East has experienced turmoil since the
seventh century, when the death of the Prophet Muhammad led
to bitter Sunni-Shiite battles over who should lead the Muslim
community, the modern source of trouble can be traced back to
the birth of Israel as a sovereign nation in 1948. Anti-Semitism and

legitimate grievances in regard to living space and independence have led to assassinations, terrorism, and war.

Not that the significant struggles facing the countries of that area and beyond revolve solely around that Jewish state. The various religious and political factions throughout the Middle East, as well as the heads of their generally theocratic governments, have caused death and destruction in Iraq, Iran, Syria, and many other nations. And though some have cited Israel as a center of regional discord, only Iranian and Palestinians leaders in most recent years have threatened that country militarily.

When dissecting the differences between the Middle East and the rest of the world in an attempt to explain its volatility, many cite religious extremism and theocracy. The intensity in which many embrace their religious beliefs has led to intolerance against those of others. Governments that create laws based on their perceptions of strict adherence to religion seem destined to foment violence when they conflict with the views of religious zealots on the other side.

That view is borne out by modern history, whether it has been conflict involving the right of Israel to exist—which many contend has been as strongly a religious issue as it is a political one—or civil wars between religious in other parts of the Middle East. The first salvo was fired soon after the state of Israel was proclaimed, when it repelled an invasion of neighboring states, causing about 700,000 Arabs to flee. The result was that Israel occupied a larger land mass than the United Nations had proposed.

The Jewish state has remained a source of conflict ever since. The founding of the Palestinian Liberation Army in 1964 proved a precursor to a war three years later—in which Israel showed its military strength by defeating Egypt in just six days and wrested from its enemy the Sinai and Gaza strip, as well as the West Bank and East Jerusalem from Jordan and the Golan Heights from Syria. The U.S. called for Israel to withdraw from those territories in return for Arab League recognition, to no avail. The Arabs refused to recognize or even negotiate with Israel.

Attempts to bring peace since then have proven futile. The United Nations allowed the PLO to represent their Palestinian people in 1974, but their inclusion simply highlighted the inability of that body to make a difference in the Middle East. Egyptian leader Anwar Sadat was assassinated in 1981, three years after he boldly signed the Camp David Accords in an attempt to bring peace and stability.

Modern Middle Eastern history has been marked by many events, few of which can be termed positive or encouraging. In 1972, a Palestinian terrorist group that called itself Black September murdered the Israeli team, turning the Munich Olympics into a tragedy. In 1979, a band of Iranian students took 52 American diplomats hostage. From 1980 to 1989, a war between Iran and Iraq resulted in more than one million casualties. In 1990, that same country invaded and brutalized tiny Kuwait, leading to the Gulf War. In 2001, terrorists hijacked planes that crashed into the World Trade Center in New York and the Pentagon in Washington, killing thousands. The American invasion of Iraq, leading to the rise of Al Qaeda and ISIS, has since caused more terrorist attacks around the world, as well as a civil war and humanitarian crisis in Syria that has resulted in an estimated 400,000 dead.

The death and destruction lead some to believe there is no chance for lasting peace. Others feel that events such as the Arab Spring of 2011, which included popular uprisings in Libya, Egypt, Yemen, Syria, and Iraq by those seeking more democratic forms of government, show a rising tide of change in the region. *Viewpoints in Modern World History: Peace in the Middle East* discusses both the harsh and hopeful sides of this complex issue.

A Historical Perspective

Preface

Nineteenth and 20th century philosopher and essayist George Santayana famously stated that those who fail to learn from history are condemned to repeat it. One can argue that such has not been the case in regard to the centuries of political and religious upheaval in the Middle East. It would be almost impossible not to learn from that much history, yet the turmoil never subsides. In fact, the advent of terrorism and nuclear ambitions in recent decades has served to make the situation in the region more dangerous than ever.

However, gaining a knowledge of Middle Eastern history—particularly since the establishment of the Jewish state of Israel following the horrors of the Holocaust and World War II—is a necessary step toward understanding the myriad issues involved. Dozens of noteworthy, and mostly disturbing, events that have occurred since the late 1940s have shaped the current state of the Middle East. And though many of them have revolved around the stalemate between Israel and the Palestinians, others involved the former only in periphery.

The Middle East has remained the most consistently violent and volatile area on the planet, greatly due to the theocracies that have tied religion to law and religious zealots that have resorted to terrorism to express their intolerance. The result has been attacks and wars. Blood has been spilled on the battlefields to maintain Israeli strength and independence in such conflicts as the Six-Day War (1967) and for various political and religious reasons in Iraq and Afghanistan since the turn of the 21st century. The era has also been marked by horrific single events, such as the slaying of Israeli athletes at the 1972 Summer Olympics in Munich and the assassination of Egyptian leader Anwar Sadat nine years later. Bombings and other terrorist actions are seemingly weekly—if not daily—occurrences in the Middle East.

The peace-loving people of the world and, specifically those in the Middle East, including the spate of refugees that have been driven from the homes, live more in the present than the past. They tend to gloss over history when seeking solutions to the endless overwhelming violence. But the words of warning expressed by Santayana ring as true today as they ever have. Only through history can one understand the concerns and motivations of those with the power to turn peace from a pipe dream into a reality.

Digging for the Roots of the Conflict

Aras Ahmed Mhamad

The following viewpoint from freelance journalist Aras Ahmed Mhamad insists that current political systems of theocracy and dictatorships in the Middle East cannot be sustained if peace is to become a reality. He argues that religious intolerance and fundamentalism must also be eliminated in any attempt to bring stability to the region. He also states that free and fair elections are necessary to empower the people. Mhamad is founder and deputy editor of SMART, *an independent English magazine that centers its focus on literature and society. He has contributed to* Fair Observer, *the* World Weekly, *and* Newsweek Middle East.

One fundamental problem for Middle Eastern countries is that a majority of the rulers are illegitimate. While each country has its own history and trajectory, common patterns prevail across the region: Those in power have not received their positions from a fair and transparent electoral process. They see themselves as above the law and misuse their absolute power.

These autocrats act as a guardian of the people or treat them as an enemy. Sets of tribal and religious convictions replace law in many countries in the Middle East and North Africa, and power is fundamentally linked to tribalism or religion.

How have power struggles, religious conflict, discrimination, security issues, colonialism and Western hegemony, values and

"The Roots of Conflict in the Middle East," by Aras Ahmed Mhamad, Fair Observer, September 28, 2015. Reprinted by Permission.

intervention shaped the Middle East? This author spoke to PhD students, academics and university lecturers to learn more.

Muhammad Waladbagi, a PhD candidate at Durham University working on Turkey-Iraqi Kurdistan relations, states that the modern history of the Middle East has witnessed frequent interstate wars, numerous revolutions, coup d'états, civil wars and economic problems:

> *"These are signs of fundamental problems in the region's political culture that at times has set the ruling regimes against their people. It is quite difficult to identify and explain the reasons behind such phenomena in a few sentences as the origins of the problems differ in each specific case, and Middle Eastern states are not homogeneous as they have many differences."*

The Role of Religion

The feeling of attachment to tribalism and fake patriotism under the umbrella of religion is stronger and more apparent than respect for human rights and pluralism in the Middle East. Patriotism is used as a tool to accumulate wealth and oppress the rights of minorities, while religion and tribalism are often militarized, making the use of violence legitimate and normal.

Sabir Hasan, a lecturer at the University of Human Development and a PhD student at the University of Leeds, says religion—specifically Islam—is an inseparable part of Middle Eastern society, and it is one of the most influential domains of Kurdish social life:

> *"It is not surprising that different tribal and so-called patriotic groups resort to religion to gain legacy and popularity. As for 'fake patriotism', as you termed it, we need a simple glance at the contemporary history of Middle Eastern regimes, including Kurdistan, to see what abuses and scandals have been committed in the name of patriotism. It is axiomatic that those who first claimed to be loyal patriots have eventually become millionaires, all at the expense of the public. Those who misuse religion and patriotism can be regarded, at best, as opportunists."*

In a region where exchange of power often causes destruction and chaos, the psychology of the rulers is structured in such a way that they consider themselves to always be right, thus there is no need for an election. Humans are not seen as humans, but as either friend or foe. Ironically, one has to act like an enemy to be a friend and a friend to be an enemy. That is to say, one has to be the enemy of freedom to be the friend of an oppressor, and to be a protector of an oppressor to be the enemy of democracy.

Power Struggles

Analyzing the issue of power struggles from a psychoanalytic perspective, Mohammed Akoi, an assistant lecturer in Raparin University in Sulaymaniyah, says:

"Sigmund Freud talks in detail about the Oedipus complex; that is, the unconscious rivalry between the father and the son. I see a similar type of complex when it comes to rulers in the Middle East. There is a myth in Kurdish folklore that could say a lot about father-son rivalry in the Middle-Eastern context.

"The story goes that a father, after having lost all his sons but one, arranges a wedding for his last son, Saidawan. As the party ends, Saidawan goes hunting to the mountains, and so does his father. Saidawan dresses in a wild goat's clothing in order to attract other goats and thus hunt them. His father, on the other hand, seeing a supposed wild goat and not knowing it is his son in disguise, kills him and thus loses his last son.

"The story is often told as a tragic misfortune on the part of the father. However, approaching the incident from a Freudian interpretation, it is the father who kills his son unconsciously. Much has been said about the Middle Eastern father as an example of divine authority who is always there to punish the son."

Akoi argues that rulers in the Middle East play the role of a typical superior who enjoys the authority of the father. Therefore, it comes as no surprise that democracy, the product of Western consciousness, always fails to shake the Middle Eastern father's position.

The dictators of Middle Eastern countries see armed struggle as a pathway to their eternal need for power. Instead of promoting coexistence, they embrace war and military confrontation; instead of building legitimate institutions, they destroy the country's infrastructure; and instead of organizing an inclusive, lawful military force, they establish militia units for the sake of adding fuel to the sectarian disputes. This paves the way for the dictators to remain in power as long as they want or until they are forcefully deposed.

For Sarkawt Shamsulddin, a political analyst at the Kurdish Policy Foundation specializing in governance and security and NRT TV's bureau chief in Washington DC, two issues are of pivotal importance: the abuse of religion and a lack of good governance. The focus here is on governance.

> "*The rulers in the Middle East have been oppressing their people for decades and they have used different means to do so, such as undermining human rights, democracy, freedom of speech and civil society as a whole. They have undermined opposition groups. They have mostly invested in military and security institutions. Therefore, when revolutions or what is called the 'Arab Spring' emerged, they use their military capability to stay in power.*"

In the underdeveloped countries of the Middle East, security and military forces are dominated and ruled by tribal chiefs and religious figures. Infringement of political rights is authorized through elastic rules, and the confiscation of democratic values is fallaciously considered a religious duty. The public sphere is in total chaos, and the government has too much influence through the media, economy, education and even on the private lives of the people. This abuse of power has become an inherent part of governments' mechanism to uproot any kind of freedom—be it freedom of speech, freedom of expression, freedom of conscience or freedom of the press.

Zubir Rasool, a PhD candidate of Middle East politics at the University of Exeter, argues that there are numerous problematic issues that can contribute to the structure of current conflict in the Middle East. The main issue in this regard has to do with the structure of the so-called "nation-state" on the one hand, and its political, social and economic functions on the other hand.

"The evolution of the nation-state did not come from a natural process in the Middle East. Large groups of Middle Eastern countries were the results of colonial operations—whether it was from the Ottoman Empire or European colonialism. Both of these historical moments' legacies share a responsibility for the creative chaos in the Middle East nowadays. The terms nation-building or state-building was just a figurative cover for the combination of different ethnic, tribal, linguistic and cultural identities. The legacy of the Ottoman Empire is based on the distinction between Muslims and non-Muslims; also, non-Muslims were divided among their ethnicities and religious sects."

The middle-class has deteriorated and the professional workforce is almost non-existent. A lack of public facilities, low income and high unemployment keep people frustrated. A lack of food quality and stable electricity, poor health care and stagnant education keep people over-occupied and struggling. This way, people do not have the means to revolt. They are more occupied with providing the basic needs to survive, let alone the strenuous dangers of migration and the perpetual challenges of resettlement, identity, discrimination and cultural integration.

Refugees

Ramyar Hassani, a human rights observer in Latin America, Europe and Kurdistan, says that in a Middle East that is burning because of sectarian wars and extremist organizations, being a refugee has become a normal phenomenon.

"On the one hand, the proxy wars of regional powers have forced thousands of Middle Easterners to flee and leave everything behind. On the other hand, the wrong policies of Western and world powers led the Middle East into a clash of extremists, which resulted in thousands of refugees [heading] to a safer country [and] dreaming of a life without violence."

With that in mind, whenever there is a revolution, the faces change, but the mentalities are the same. That is to say, a new despotic clan will take over power, establishing the same sort of mechanism to replace and then rule in the same manner as the ousted autocrat. Each clan or tribe controls a certain territory with their own armed force and militia in hand and their own rules in place.

That being said, constitutional legitimacy is threatened by political outbidding and revolution. The legitimate exchange or handover of power and social justice are vulnerable in the face of political and economic corruption, which is why disorder, instability and war have always been part of the autocrat's culture and mentality.

Sherko Kirmanj, a visiting senior lecturer at the University of Utara Malaysia and the author of *Identity and Nation in Iraq*, believes the question of legitimacy is one problem that faces the Middle East.

"One of the major problems confronting Middle Eastern societies is that the process of modernity in the region is not home-grown, but rather an imposed one. Modernity with all its dimensions and outcomes, including the nation-state, secularism, democratization, freedom, etc, were alien concepts introduced into Middle Eastern societies in the late 19th and early 20th centuries. The introduction of these concepts and the values that embrace such equality, justice, fairness, freedom of speech and freedom of religion—just to name a few—led to a clash with local and traditional values of these societies."

In the End

Western leaders and institutions have a limited understanding and familiarity with Middle Eastern societies, cultures and politics. This often leads to a focus on increasing arms and ammunition supplies and offering military training, especially in times of a violent insurgency, instead of the much-needed humanitarian, educational and developmental aid. This creates an ongoing cycle, wherein whoever has the most military strength holds power and steps into the same pattern of governmental rule.

What has blinded the West is the age-old misconception that Middle Eastern societies are anti-civil society, anti-democracy and anti-multiculturalism. This thinking leads to the conclusion that these societies are doomed to remain in bloodshed, where the best treatment is the importing of more and more weapons. This approach fails to address the root problems and instead contributes to the cycle of violence.

The West must realize that the real danger lies in the empowerment of religious fanatics and systemic corruption that have replaced true critical thinking, quality education and effective institutions.

By publishing and glamorizing radical groups' propaganda on media platforms such as YouTube, the West can demonstrate how significant a culture of diversity and rule of law is for consolidating democracy. These two elements—rule of law and a culture of diversity—are the only means through which autocracy and religious fundamentalism can be overthrown.

Taking a Time Machine to the Birth of Israel

Alison Weir

Journalist Alison Weir asserts in the following viewpoint that only through a thorough exploration of the circumstances surrounding the establishment of the Jewish state of Israel in 1947 and 1948 can we understand modern Middle Eastern history—particularly the desire of the Palestinians for recognition by Israel and the United Nations. Weir is executive director of If Americans Knew, a nonprofit organization that seeks to provide Americans with information on important topics underreported by the nation's media outlets. Weir also serves on the board of directors of the Council for the National Interest.

To better understand the Palestinian bid for membership in the United Nations, it is important to understand the original 1947 UN action on Israel-Palestine

The common representation of Israel's birth is that the UN created Israel, that the world was in favor of this move, and that the US governmental establishment supported it. All these assumptions are demonstrably incorrect.

In reality, while the UN General Assembly recommended the creation of a Jewish state in part of Palestine, that recommendation was non-binding and never implemented by the Security Council.

Second, the General Assembly passed that recommendation only after Israel proponents threatened and bribed numerous countries in order to gain a required two-thirds of votes.

"The Real Story of How Israel Was Created," by Alison Weir, If Americans Knew, October 11, 2011. Reprinted by Permission.

Third, the US administration supported the recommendation out of domestic electoral considerations, and took this position over the strenuous objections of the State Department, the CIA, and the Pentagon.

The passage of the General Assembly recommendation sparked increased violence in the region. Over the following months the armed wing of the pro-Israel movement, which had long been preparing for war, perpetrated a series of massacres and expulsions throughout Palestine, implementing a plan to clear the way for a majority-Jewish state.

It was this armed aggression, and the ethnic cleansing of at least three-quarters of a million indigenous Palestinians, that created the Jewish state on land that had been 95 percent non-Jewish prior to Zionist immigration and that even after years of immigration remained 70 percent non-Jewish. And despite the shallow patina of legality its partisans extracted from the General Assembly, Israel was born over the opposition of American experts and of governments around the world, who opposed it on both pragmatic and moral grounds.

Let us look at the specifics.

Background of the UN Partition Recommendation

In 1947 the UN took up the question of Palestine, a territory that was then administered by the British.

Approximately 50 years before, a movement called political Zionism had begun in Europe. Its intention was to create a Jewish state in Palestine through pushing out the Christian and Muslim inhabitants who made up over 95 percent of its population and replacing them with Jewish immigrants.

As this colonial project grew through subsequent years, the indigenous Palestinians reacted with occasional bouts of violence; Zionists had anticipated this since people usually resist being expelled from their land. In various written documents cited by numerous Palestinian and Israeli historians, they discussed their strategy: they would buy up the land until all the previous inhabitants had emigrated, or, failing this, use violence to force them out.

When the buy-out effort was able to obtain only a few percent of the land, Zionists created a number of terrorist groups to fight against both the Palestinians and the British. Terrorist and future Israeli Prime Minister Menachem Begin later bragged that Zionists had brought terrorism both to the Middle East and to the world at large.

Finally, in 1947 the British announced that they would be ending their control of Palestine, which had been created through the League of Nations following World War One, and turned the question of Palestine over to the United Nations.

At this time, the Zionist immigration and buyout project had increased the Jewish population of Palestine to 30 percent and land ownership from 1 percent to approximately 6 percent.

Since a founding principle of the UN was "self-determination of peoples," one would have expected to the UN to support fair, democratic elections in which inhabitants could create their own independent country.

Instead, Zionists pushed for a General Assembly resolution in which they would be given a disproportionate 55 percent of Palestine. (While they rarely announced this publicly, their stated plan was to later take the rest of Palestine.)

U.S. Officials Oppose Partition Plan

The U.S. State Department opposed this partition plan strenuously, considering Zionism contrary to both fundamental American principles and US interests.

Author Donald Neff reports that Loy Henderson, Director of the State Department's Office of Near Eastern and African Affairs, wrote a memo to the Secretary of State warning:

> *"...support by the Government of the United States of a policy favoring the setting up of a Jewish State in Palestine would be contrary to the wishes of a large majority of the local inhabitants with respect to their form of government. Furthermore, it would*

*have a strongly adverse effect upon American interests throughout
the Near and Middle East..."*

Henderson went on to emphasize:

*"At the present time the United States has a moral prestige in
the Near and Middle East unequaled by that of any other great
power. We would lose that prestige and would be likely for many
years to be considered as a betrayer of the high principles which
we ourselves have enunciated during the period of the war."*

When Zionists began pushing for a partition plan through
the UN, Henderson recommended strongly against supporting
their proposal. He warned that such a partition would have to be
implemented by force and emphasized that it was "not based on
any principle." He went on to write: "...[partition] would guarantee
that the Palestine problem would be permanent and still more
complicated in the future..."

Henderson specifically pointed out:

*"...[proposals for partition] are in definite contravention to various
principles laid down in the [UN] Charter as well as to principles
on which American concepts of Government are based. These
proposals, for instance, ignore such principles as self-determination
and majority rule. They recognize the principle of a theocratic
racial state and even go so far in several instances as to discriminate
on grounds of religion and race..."*

Henderson was far from alone in making his recommendations.
He wrote that his views were not only those of the entire Near East
Division but were shared by "nearly every member of the Foreign
Service or of the Department who has worked to any appreciable
extent on Near Eastern problems."

Henderson wasn't exaggerating. Official after official and
agency after agency opposed Zionism.

In 1947 the CIA reported that Zionist leadership was pursuing
objectives that would endanger both Jews and "the strategic
interests of the Western powers in the Near and Middle East."

Truman Accedes to Pro-Israel Lobby

President Harry Truman, however, ignored this advice. Truman's political advisor, Clark Clifford, believed that the Jewish vote and contributions were essential to winning the upcoming presidential election, and that supporting the partition plan would garner that support. (Truman's opponent, Dewey, took similar stands for similar reasons.)

Truman's Secretary of State George Marshall, the renowned World War II General and author of the Marshall Plan, was furious to see electoral considerations taking precedence over policies based on national interest. He condemned what he called a "transparent dodge to win a few votes," which would cause "[t]he great dignity of the office of President [to be] seriously diminished."

Marshall wrote that the counsel offered by Clifford "was based on domestic political considerations, while the problem which confronted us was international. I said bluntly that if the President were to follow Mr. Clifford's advice and if in the elections I were to vote, I would vote against the President..."

Henry F. Grady, who has been called "America's top diplomatic soldier for a critical period of the Cold War," headed a 1946 commission aimed at coming up with a solution for Palestine. Grady later wrote about the Zionist lobby and its damaging effect on US national interests.

Grady argued that without Zionist pressure, the U.S. would not have had "the ill-will with the Arab states, which are of such strategic importance in our 'cold war' with the soviets." He also described the decisive power of the lobby:

> *"I have had a good deal of experience with lobbies but this group started where those of my experience had ended..... I have headed a number of government missions but in no other have I ever experienced so much disloyalty"...... "in the United States, since there is no political force to counterbalance Zionism, its campaigns are apt to be decisive."*

Former Undersecretary of State Dean Acheson also opposed Zionism. Acheson's biographer writes that Acheson "worried that the West would pay a high price for Israel." Another Author, John Mulhall, records Acheson's warning:

> *"...to transform [Palestine] into a Jewish State capable of receiving a million or more immigrants would vastly exacerbate the political problem and imperil not only American but all Western interests in the Near East."*

Secretary of Defense James Forrestal also tried, unsuccessfully, to oppose the Zionists. He was outraged that Truman's Mideast policy was based on what he called "squalid political purposes," asserting that "United States policy should be based on United States national interests and not on domestic political considerations."

Forrestal represented the general Pentagon view when he said that "no group in this country should be permitted to influence our policy to the point where it could endanger our national security."

A report by the National Security Council warned that the Palestine turmoil was acutely endangering the security of the United States. A CIA report stressed the strategic importance of the Middle East and its oil resources.

Similarly, George F. Kennan, the State Department's Director of Policy Planning, issued a top-secret document on January 19, 1947 that outlined the enormous damage done to the US by the partition plan ("Report by the Policy Planning Staff on Position of the United States with Respect to Palestine").

Kennan cautioned that "important U.S. oil concessions and air base rights" could be lost through US support for partition and warned that the USSR stood to gain by the partition plan.

Kermit Roosevelt, Teddy Roosevelt's nephew and a legendary intelligence agent, was another who was deeply disturbed by events, noting:

> *"The process by which Zionist Jews have been able to promote American support for the partition of Palestine demonstrates the vital need of a foreign policy based on national rather than partisan interests... Only when the national interests of the United States, in*

their highest terms, take precedence over all other considerations, can a logical, farseeing foreign policy be evolved. No American political leader has the right to compromise American interests to gain partisan votes..."

He went on:

"The present course of world crisis will increasingly force upon Americans the realization that their national interests and those of the proposed Jewish state in Palestine are going to conflict. It is to be hoped that American Zionists and non-Zionists alike will come to grips with the realities of the problem."

The head of the State Department's Division of Near Eastern Affairs, Gordon P. Merriam, warned against the partition plan on moral grounds:

"U.S. support for partition of Palestine as a solution to that problem can be justified only on the basis of Arab and Jewish consent. Otherwise we should violate the principle of self-determination which has been written into the Atlantic Charter, the declaration of the United Nations, and the United Nations Charter–a principle that is deeply embedded in our foreign policy. Even a United Nations determination in favor of partition would be, in the absence of such consent, a stultification and violation of UN's own charter."

Merriam added that without consent, "bloodshed and chaos" would follow, a tragically accurate prediction.

An internal State Department memorandum accurately predicted how Israel would be born through armed aggression masked as defense:

"...the Jews will be the actual aggressors against the Arabs. However, the Jews will claim that they are merely defending the boundaries of a state which were traced by the UN...In the event of such Arab outside aid the Jews will come running to the Security Council with the claim that their state is the object of armed aggression and will use every means to obscure the fact that it is their own armed aggression against the Arabs inside which is the cause of Arab counter-attack."

And American Vice Consul William J. Porter foresaw another outcome of the partition plan: that no Arab State would actually ever come to be in Palestine.

Pro-Israel Pressure on General Assembly Members

When it was clear that the Partition recommendation did not have the required two-thirds of the UN General Assembly to pass, Zionists pushed through a delay in the vote. They then used this period to pressure numerous nations into voting for the recommendation. A number of people later described this campaign.

Robert Nathan, a Zionist who had worked for the US government and who was particularly active in the Jewish Agency, wrote afterward, "We used any tools at hand," such as telling certain delegations that the Zionists would use their influence to block economic aid to any countries that did not vote the right way.

Another Zionist proudly stated: "Every clue was meticulously checked and pursued. Not the smallest or the remotest of nations, but was contacted and wooed. Nothing was left to chance."

Financier and longtime presidential advisor Bernard Baruch told France it would lose U.S. aid if it voted against partition. Top White House executive assistant David Niles organized pressure on Liberia; rubber magnate Harvey Firestone pressured Liberia.

Latin American delegates were told that the Pan-American highway construction project would be more likely if they voted yes. Delegates' wives received mink coats (the wife of the Cuban delegate returned hers); Costa Rica's President Jose Figueres reportedly received a blank checkbook. Haiti was promised economic aid if it would change its original vote opposing partition.

Longtime Zionist Supreme Court Justice Felix Frankfurter, along with ten senators and Truman domestic advisor Clark Clifford, threatened the Philippines (seven bills were pending on the Philippines in Congress).

Before the vote on the plan, the Philippine delegate had given a passionate speech against partition, defending the inviolable "primordial rights of a people to determine their political future and to preserve the territorial integrity of their native land..."

He went on to say that he could not believe that the General Assembly would sanction a move that would place the world "back on the road to the dangerous principles of racial exclusiveness and to the archaic documents of theocratic governments."

Twenty-four hours later, after intense Zionist pressure, the delegate voted in favor of partition.

The U.S. delegation to the U.N. was so outraged when Truman insisted that they support partition that the State Department director of U.N. Affairs was sent to New York to prevent the delegates from resigning en masse.

On Nov 29, 1947 the partition resolution, 181, passed. While this resolution is frequently cited, it was of limited (if any) legal impact. General Assembly resolutions, unlike Security Council resolutions, are not binding on member states. For this reason, the resolution requested that "[t]he Security Council take the necessary measures as provided for in the plan for its implementation," which the Security Council never did. Legally, the General Assembly Resolution was a "recommendation" and did not create any states.

What it did do, however, was increase the fighting in Palestine. Within months (and before Israel dates the beginning of its founding war) the Zionists had forced out 413,794 people. Zionist military units had stealthily been preparing for war before the UN vote and had acquired massive weaponry, some of it through a widespread network of illicit gunrunning operations in the US under a number of front groups.

The UN eventually managed to create a temporary and very partial ceasefire. A Swedish UN mediator who had previously rescued thousands of Jews from the Nazis was dispatched to negotiate an end to the violence. Israeli assassins killed him and Israel continued what it was to call its "war of independence."

At the end of this war, through a larger military force than that of its adversaries and the ruthless implementation of plans to push out as many non-Jews as possible, Israel came into existence on 78 percent of Palestine.

At least 33 massacres of Palestinian civilians were perpetrated, half of them before a single Arab army had entered the conflict, hundreds of villages were depopulated and razed, and a team of cartographers was sent out to give every town, village, river, and hillock a new, Hebrew name. All vestiges of Palestinian habitation, history, and culture were to be erased from history, an effort that almost succeeded.

Israel, which claims to be the "only democracy in the Middle East," decided not to declare official borders or to write a constitution, a situation which continues to this day. In 1967 it took still more Palestinian and Syrian land, which is now illegally occupied territory, since the annexation of land through military conquest is outlawed by modern international law. It has continued this campaign of growth through armed acquisition and illegal confiscation of land ever since.

Individual Israelis, like Palestinians and all people, are legally and morally entitled to an array of human rights.

On the other hand, the state of Israel's vaunted "right to exist" is based on an alleged "right" derived from might, an outmoded concept that international legal conventions do not recognize, and in fact specifically prohibit.

How a Refugee Crisis Gave Rise to a Jewish State

The United States Holocaust Memorial Museum

The United States Holocaust Memorial Museum provides historical reasoning behind the justification for a strong Israeli state in the following viewpoint, which revisits the horrors of the systematic murder of Jews during World War II by the Nazi regime. The arguments against the existence of a Jewish state made by some in the Middle East, including a regime in Iran that has expressed a desire to wipe the country off the map, must be countered by an understanding of the genocide that killed off six million Jews during the war. The museum seeks to keep the memories forever alive so that it will never be forgotten.

D uring World War II, the Nazis deported between seven and nine million Europeans, mostly to Germany. Within months of Germany's surrender in May 1945, the Allies repatriated to their home countries more than six million displaced persons (DPs; wartime refugees). Between 1.5 million and two million DPs refused repatriation.

Most Jewish survivors, who had survived concentration camps or had been in hiding, were unable or unwilling to return to eastern Europe because of postwar antisemitism and the destruction of their communities during the Holocaust. Many of those who did return feared for their lives. In Poland, for example, locals initiated several violent pogroms. The worst was the one in Kielce in 1946 in

"Postwar Refugee Crisis and the Establishment of the State of Israel," United States Holocaust Memorial Museum. Reprinted by Permission.

which 42 Jews, all survivors of the Holocaust, were killed. These pogroms led to a significant second movement of Jewish refugees from Poland to the west.

Many Holocaust survivors moved westward to territories liberated by the western Allies. They were housed in displaced persons camps and urban displaced persons centers. The Allies established such camps in Allied-occupied Germany, Austria, and Italy for refugees waiting to leave Europe. Most of the Jewish displaced persons were in the British occupation zone in northern Germany and in the American occupation zone in the south. The British established a large displaced persons camp adjacent to the former concentration camp of Bergen-Belsen in Germany. Several large camps holding 4,000 to 6,000 displaced persons each—Feldafing, Landsberg, and Foehrenwald—were located in the American zone.

At its peak in 1947, the Jewish displaced person population reached approximately 250,000. While the United Nations Relief and Rehabilitation Administration (UNRRA) administered all of the displaced persons camps and centers, Jewish displaced persons achieved a large measure of internal autonomy.

A variety of Jewish agencies were active in the displaced persons camps. The American Jewish Joint Distribution Committee provided refugees with food and clothing, and the Organization for Rehabilitation through Training (ORT) offered vocational training. Jewish displaced persons also formed self-governing organizations, and many worked toward the establishment of a Jewish state in Palestine. There were central committees of Jewish displaced persons in the American and British zones which, as their primary goals, pressed for greater immigration opportunities and the creation of a Jewish homeland in Palestine.

In the United States, immigration restrictions strictly limited the number of refugees permitted to enter the country. The British, who had received a mandate from the League of Nations to administer Palestine, severely restricted Jewish immigration there largely because of Arab objections. Many countries closed their borders to immigration. Despite these obstacles, many Jewish displaced persons attempted to leave Europe as soon as possible.

The Jewish Brigade Group, formed as a unit within the British army in late 1944, worked with former partisans to help organize the Brihah (literally "escape"), the exodus of 250,000 Jewish refugees across closed borders from inside Europe to the coast in an attempt to sail for Palestine. The Mosad le-Aliyah Bet, an agency established by the Jewish leadership in Palestine, organized "illegal" immigration (Aliyah Bet) by ship. However, the British intercepted most of the ships.

In 1947, for example, the British stopped the *Exodus 1947* at the port of Haifa. The ship had 4,500 Holocaust survivors on board, who were returned to Germany on British vessels. In most cases, the British detained the refugees—over 50,000—in detention camps on the island of Cyprus in the eastern Mediterranean Sea. The British use of detention camps as a deterrent failed, and the flood of immigrants attempting entry into Palestine continued.

The internment of Jewish refugees—many of them Holocaust survivors—turned world opinion against British policy in Palestine. The report of the Anglo-American Commission of Inquiry in January 1946 led US president Harry Truman to pressure Britain into admitting 100,000 Jewish refugees into Palestine.

As the crisis escalated, the British government decided to submit the problem of Palestine to the United Nations (UN). In a special session, the UN General Assembly voted on November 29, 1947, to partition Palestine into two new states, one Jewish and the other Arab, a recommendation that Jewish leaders accepted and the Arabs rejected.

After the British began the withdrawal of their military forces from Palestine in early April 1948, Zionist leaders moved to establish a modern Jewish state. On May 14, 1948, David Ben-Gurion, the chairman of the Jewish Agency for Palestine, announced the formation of the state of Israel, declaring, "The Nazi Holocaust, which engulfed millions of Jews in Europe, proved anew the urgency of the reestablishment of the Jewish State, which would solve the problem of Jewish homelessness by opening the gates to all Jews and lifting the Jewish people to equality in the family of nations."

Holocaust survivors from displaced persons camps in Europe and from detention camps on Cyprus were welcomed into the Jewish homeland. Many of them fought in Israel's War of Independence in 1948 and 1949. In 1953, Yad Vashem (The Martyrs' and Heroes' Remembrance Authority), the national institution for Holocaust commemoration, was established.

Tracing History to Tell a Different Story

Matti Friedman

The author of Sami Rohr Prize winner The Aleppo Codex (2014) and many articles about Israel and Middle Eastern history, Matti Friedman contends in the following viewpoint that Israel was not an invader to the region when it was established as a nation in 1948, but rather the result of a people returning to their homeland, only to be met by resistance and the same intolerance that resulted in mass murder during the Holocaust. Friedman insists that any other view of the current state of Palestinian-Israeli relations falls into the category of revisionist history and must be rejected.

On May 15, many in the Arab world and elsewhere mark the Nakba, or the "Catastrophe," mourning the displacement of the Palestinian Arabs during the 1948 war with Israel. This year, as always, the commemoration will obscure the collapse at the same time of a different Arab society that few remember.

I have spent a great deal of time in the past four years interviewing people born and raised in Aleppo, Syria. Some of these people, most of whom are now in their eighties, are descended from families with roots in Aleppo going back more than two millennia, to Roman times. None of them lives there now.

On November 30, 1947, a day after the United Nations voted to partition Palestine into two states, one for Arabs and one for Jews, Aleppo erupted. Mobs stalked Jewish neighborhoods,

"A Different History of Displacement and Loss," by Matti Friedman, The Times of Israel, May 15, 2012. Reprinted by Permission. Originally appeared in The Times of Israel. www.timesofisrael.com.

looting houses and burning synagogues; one man I interviewed remembered fleeing his home, a barefoot nine-year-old, moments before it was set on fire. Abetted by the government, the rioters burned 50 Jewish shops, five schools, 18 synagogues and an unknown number of homes. The next day the Jewish community's wealthiest families fled, and in the following months the rest began sneaking out in small groups, most of them headed to the new state of Israel. They forfeited their property, and faced imprisonment or torture if they were caught. Some disappeared en route. But the risk seemed worthwhile: in Damascus, the capital, rioters killed 13 Jews, including eight children, in August 1948, and there were similar events in other Arab cities.

At the time of the UN vote, there were about 10,000 Jews in Aleppo. By the mid-1950s there were 2,000, living in fear of the security forces and the mob. By the early 1990s no more than a handful remained, and today there are none. Similar scripts played out across the Islamic world. Some 850,000 Jews were forced from their homes.

If we are to fully understand the Israel-Arab conflict, the memory of these people and their exodus must be acknowledged— not as a political weapon, a negotiating tactic or as part of a competition about who suffered more, but simply as history without which it is impossible to understand Israel and the way the Arab world sees it.

Everyone knows the Palestinian refugees are part of the equation of Mideast peace, and anyone who is interested can visit a Palestinian refugee camp and hear true and wrenching stories of expulsion and loss. Among the Jews expelled by Arabs, on the other hand, one can find few who think of themselves as refugees or define themselves by their dispossession. Most are citizens of Israel.

Of the 20 families in my fairly average Jerusalem apartment building, half are in Israel because of the Arab expulsion of Jews, and that is representative of Israel as a whole. According to the Israeli demographer Sergio dellaPergola of Hebrew University, though intermarriage over two or three generations has muddled the statistics, roughly half of the 6 million Jews in Israel today came from the Muslim world or are descended from people who did. Many Arabs, and many Israelis, consider Israel a Western enclave in the Middle East. But these numbers do not support that view.

These Jews have shaped Israel and are a key force in the country's political life. They also make Israel very different from the American Jewish community, which is overwhelmingly rooted in Europe. They are a pillar of Israel's right wing, particularly of the Likud party. They maintain a wary view of Israel's neighbors—a view that has been strengthened by the actions of the Palestinians but that is rooted in their own historical experience and in what might be considered an instinctive understanding of the region's unkind realities.

The legacy of their exodus in the countries they left behind is harder to detect, but it, too, is significant.

In many Arab towns and cities there is an area where Jews used to live. In some cities, like Cairo, this area is still called *harat al-yahud*, the Jewish Quarter. Reporting there several years ago I found people who could show me the location of a certain abandoned synagogue, which they knew by name. A man who once showed me around Fez, Morocco, knew exactly where the old Jewish neighborhood, the *mellah*, had been, though there was not a single Jew there and had not been for many years. There are remnants like this in Aleppo, Tripoli, Baghdad and elsewhere. The people who live in or around the Jews' old homes still know who used to own them and how they left; this extinct Jewish world might have been forgotten elsewhere, but millions in the Arab world see evidence of it every day.

As I have reported this nearly invisible story, it has occured to me that we often hate most the things or people that remind us of something we dislike about ourselves, and that here lies one of the hidden dynamics of the Israel-Arab conflict. It is one papered over by the simple narrative of Nakba Day, which posits that a foreign implant displaced a native community in 1948 and that the Palestinian Arabs are paying the price for the European

Holocaust. This narrative, chiefly designed to appeal to Western guilt, also conveniently erases the uncomfortable truth that half of Israel's Jews are there not because of the Nazis but because of the Arabs themselves.

Israel is not as foreign to the Middle East as many of its neighbors like to pretend, and more than one native community was displaced in 1948. If many in the Arab world insist, as they do each Nakba Day, that Israel is a Western invader that must be repelled, it is a claim that belongs to the realm not only of politics but of psychology—one that helps repress their own knowledge that the country they try to portray as alien is also the vengeful ghost of the neighbors they wronged.

What Really Created the Iranian Hostage Crisis?

James Perloff

Prolific writer James Perloff travels back more than three decades to replant the seeds that grew into a hostage standoff between Iran and the United States. Perloff believed his article pertinent in the wake of renewed military hostilities between the two countries. In the following viewpoint, he explains why Americans should remember that the Iranian hostage crisis was sparked when the United States propped up a dishonest thief in the Shah and then gave him protection rather than allow the Iranian people to bring him to justice. Perloff's view of the Shah and his effect on the country he ruled is quite different.

A mericans have been hearing for several years about potential war with Iran. For instance, on September 17, 2006, *Time* magazine reported, "The U.S. would have to consider military action long before Iran had an actual bomb." On October 10, under the heading "A Chilling Preview of War," *Time* warned: "As Iran continues to enrich uranium, the U.S. military has issued a 'Prepare to Deploy' order."

In September 2007, *US News & World Report* stated: "Amid deepening frustration with Iran, calls for shifting Bush administration policy toward military strikes or other stronger actions are intensifying." And in June 2008, President-to-be Barack Obama declared: "The danger from Iran is grave, it is real, and my goal will be to eliminate this threat."

"Iran and the Shah: What Really Happened," by James Perloff, The New American, May 12, 2009. Reprinted by Permission of The New American.com.

However, suppose a progressive, pro-Western regime ruled Iran, representing no threat? War discussions would be unnecessary. Yet many forget that, until 30 years ago, exactly such a regime led Iran, until it was toppled with the help of the same U.S. foreign policy establishment recently beating war drums.

Meet the Shah

From 1941 until 1979, Iran was ruled by a constitutional monarchy under Mohammad Reza Pahlavi, Iran's Shah (king).

Although Iran, also called Persia, was the world's oldest empire, dating back 2,500 years, by 1900 it was floundering. Bandits dominated the land; literacy was one percent; and women, under archaic Islamic dictates, had no rights.

The Shah changed all this. Primarily by using oil-generated wealth, he modernized the nation. He built rural roads, postal services, libraries, and electrical installations. He constructed dams to irrigate Iran's arid land, making the country 90-percent self-sufficient in food production. He established colleges and universities, and at his own expense, set up an educational foundation to train students for Iran's future.

To encourage independent cultivation, the Shah donated 500,000 Crown acres to 25,000 farmers. In 1978, his last full year in power, the average Iranian earned $2,540, compared to $160 25 years earlier. Iran had full employment, requiring foreign workers. The national currency was stable for 15 years, inspiring French economist André Piettre to call Iran a country of "growth without inflation." Although Iran was the world's second largest oil exporter, the Shah planned construction of 18 nuclear power plants. He built an Olympic sports complex and applied to host the 1988 Olympics (an honor eventually assigned Seoul), an achievement unthinkable for other Middle East nations.

Long regarded as a U.S. ally, the Shah was pro-Western and anti-communist, and he was aware that he posed the main barrier to Soviet ambitions in the Middle East. As distinguished foreign-affairs analyst Hilaire du Berrier noted: "He determined to make

Iran … capable of blocking a Russian advance until the West should realize to what extent her own interests were threatened and come to his aid…. It necessitated an army of 250,000 men." The Shah's air force ranked among the world's five best. A voice for stability within the Middle East itself, he favored peace with Israel and supplied the beleaguered state with oil.

On the home front, the Shah protected minorities and permitted non-Muslims to practice their faiths. "All faith," he wrote, "imposes respect upon the beholder." The Shah also brought Iran into the 20th century by granting women equal rights. This was not to accommodate feminism, but to end archaic brutalization.

Yet, at the height of Iran's prosperity, the Shah suddenly became the target of an ignoble campaign led by U.S. and British foreign policy makers. Bolstered by slander in the Western press, these forces, along with Soviet-inspired communist insurgents, and mullahs opposing the Shah's progressiveness, combined to face him with overwhelming opposition. In three years he went from vibrant monarch to exile (on January 16, 1979), and ultimately death, while Iran fell to Ayatollah Khomeini's terror.

Houchang Nahavandi, one of the Shah's ministers and closest advisers, reveals in his book *The Last Shah of Iran*: "We now know that the idea of deposing the Shah was broached continually, from the mid-seventies on, in the National Security Council in Washington, by Henry Kissinger, whom the Shah thought of as a firm friend."

Kissinger virtually epitomized the American establishment: before acting as Secretary of State under Republicans Richard Nixon and Gerald Ford, he had been chief foreign-affairs adviser to Nelson Rockefeller, whom he called "the single most influential person in my life." Jimmy Carter defeated Ford in the 1976 presidential election, but the switch to a Democratic administration did not change the new foreign policy tilt against the Shah. Every presidential administration since Franklin D. Roosevelt's has been dominated by members of the Council on Foreign Relations (CFR), the most visible manifestation of the establishment that dictates U.S. foreign policy along internationalist lines. The Carter administration was no exception.

Nahavandi writes:

> *The alternation of parties does not change the diplomatic orientation of the United States that much. The process of toppling the Shah had been envisaged and initiated in 1974, under a certain Republican administration.... Numerous, published documents and studies bear witness to the fact, even if it was not until the beginning of the Carter administration that the decision was made to take concerted action by evoking problems related to human rights.*

The Shah's destruction required assembling a team of diplomatic "hit men." Du Berrier commented:

> *When the situation was deemed ripe, U.S. Ambassador William Sullivan — the man reputed to have toppled the pro-American government of General Phoumi Nosavan in Laos — was sent to urge the Shah to get out. In December Mr. George Ball, an instant "authority on Iran," was sent as a follow-up with the same message.*

Sullivan (CFR), a career diplomat with no Middle East experience, became our ambassador to Iran in 1977. The Shah recalled:

> *Whenever I met Sullivan and asked him to confirm these official statements [of American support], he promised he would. But a day or two later he would return, gravely shake his head, and say that he had received "no instructions" and therefore could not comment.... His answer was always the same: I have received no instructions.... This rote answer had been given me since early September [1978] and I would continue to hear it until the day I left the country.*

The other key player du Berrier named, George Ball, was a quintessential establishment man: CFR member, Bilderberger, and banker with Lehman Brothers Kuhn Loeb. The Shah commented: "What was I to make, for example, of the Administration's sudden decision to call former Under Secretary of State George Ball to the White House as an advisor on Iran? I knew that Ball was no friend."

Writes Nahavandi:

> George Ball — that guru of American diplomacy and prominento of certain think-tanks and pressure groups — once paid a long visit to Teheran, where, interestingly, the National Broadcasting Authority placed an office at his disposal. Once installed there, he played host to all the best-known dissidents and gave them encouragement. After he returned to Washington, he made public statements, hostile and insulting to the Sovereign.

Joining the smear was U.S. Senator Ted Kennedy, whose role Nahavandi recalled in a 1981 interview:

> But we must not forget the venom with which Teddy Kennedy ranted against the Shah, nor that on December 7, 1977, the Kennedy family financed a so-called committee for the defense of liberties and rights of man in Teheran, which was nothing but a headquarters for revolution.

Suddenly, the Shah noted, the U.S. media found him "a despot, an oppressor, a tyrant." Kennedy denounced him for running "one of the most violent regimes in the history of mankind."

At the center of the "human rights" complaints was the Shah's security force, SAVAK. Comparable in its mission to America's FBI, SAVAK was engaged in a deadly struggle against terrorism, most of which was fueled by the bordering USSR, which linked to Iran's internal communist party, the Tudeh. SAVAK, which had only 4,000 employees in 1978, saved many lives by averting several bombing attempts. Its prisons were open for Red Cross inspections, and though unsuccessful attempts were made on the Shah's life, he always pardoned the would-be assassins. Nevertheless, a massive campaign was deployed against him. Within Iran, Islamic fundamentalists, who resented the Shah's progressive pro-Western views, combined with Soviet-sponsored communists to overthrow the Shah. This tandem was "odd" because communism is committed to destroying *all* religion, which Marx called "the opiate of the masses." The Shah understood that "Islamic Marxism" was an oxymoron, commenting: "Of course the two concepts are irreconcilable—unless those who profess Islam do not understand their own religion or pervert it for their own political ends."

For Western TV cameras, protestors in Teheran carried empty coffins, or coffins seized from genuine funerals, proclaiming these were "victims of SAVAK." This deception—later admitted by the revolutionaries—was necessary because they had no actual martyrs to parade. Another tactic: demonstrators splashed themselves with mercurochrome, claiming SAVAK had bloodied them.

The Western media cooperated. When Carter visited Iran at the end of 1977, the press reported that his departure to Teheran International Airport had been through empty streets, because the city was "all locked up and emptied of people, by order of the SAVAK." What the media didn't mention: Carter chose to depart at 6 a.m., when the streets were naturally empty.

An equally vicious campaign occurred when the Shah and his wife, Empress Farah, came for a state visit to America in November 1977. While touring Williamsburg, Virginia, about 500 Iranian students showed up, enthusiastically applauding. However, about 50 protestors waved hammer-and-sickle red flags. These unlikely Iranians were masked, unable to speak Persian, and some were blonde. The U.S. media focused exclusively on the protesters. Wrote the Shah: "Imagine my amazement the next day when I saw the press had reversed the numbers and wrote that the fifty Shah supporters were lost in a hostile crowd."

On November 16, the Shah and Empress were due to visit Carter. Several thousand Iranian patriots surrounded the White House bearing a huge banner saying "Welcome Shah." However, as Nahavandi reports:

The police kept them as far away as possible, but allowed a small number of opponents [again, masked] to approach the railings ... close to where the Sovereign's helicopter was going to land for the official welcome. At the exact moment, when courtesies were being exchanged on the White House lawn, these people produced sticks and bicycle chains and set upon the others.... Thus, the whole world was allowed to see riotous scenes, on television, as an accompaniment to the arrival of the Imperial Couple.

Terror at Home

Two major events propelled the revolution in Iran. On the afternoon of August 19, 1978, a deliberate fire gutted the Rex Cinema in Abadan, killing 477 people, including many children with their mothers. Blocked exits prevented escape. The police learned that the fire was caused by Ruhollah Khomeini supporters, who fled to Iraq, where the ayatollah was in exile. But the international press blamed the fire on the Shah and his "dreaded SAVAK." Furthermore, the mass murder had been timed to coincide with the Shah's planned celebration of his mother's birthday; it could thus be reported that the royal family danced while Iran wept. Communist-inspired rioting swept Iran.

Foreigners, including Palestinians, appeared in the crowds. Although the media depicted demonstrations as "spontaneous uprisings," professional revolutionaries organized them. Some Iranian students were caught up in it. Here the Shah's generosity backfired. As du Berrier pointed out:

> *In his desperate need of men capable of handling the sophisticated equipment he was bringing in, the Shah had sent over a hundred thousand students abroad.... Those educated in France and America return indoctrinated by leftist professors and eager to serve as links between comrades abroad and the Communist Party at home.*

When the demonstrations turned violent, the government reluctantly invoked martial law. The second dark day was September 8. Thousands of demonstrators gathered in Teheran were ordered to disperse by an army unit. Gunmen—many on rooftops—fired on the soldiers. The Shah's army fired back. The rooftop snipers then sprayed the crowd. When the tragedy was over, 121 demonstrators and 70 soldiers and police lay dead. Autopsies revealed that most in the crowd had been killed by ammo non-regulation for the army.

Nevertheless, the Western press claimed the Shah had massacred his own people.

The Shah, extremely grieved by this incident, and wanting no further bloodshed, gave orders tightly restricting the military. This proved a mistake. Until now, the sight of his elite troops had quieted mobs. The new restraints emboldened revolutionaries, who brazenly insulted soldiers, knowing they could fire only as a last resort.

Khomeini and the Media Cabal

Meanwhile, internationalist forces rallied around a new figure they had chosen to lead Iran: Ruhollah Khomeini. A minor cleric of Indian extraction, Khomeini had denounced the Shah's reforms during the 1960s—especially women's rights and land reform for Muslim clerics, many of whom were large landholders. Because his incendiary remarks had contributed to violence and rioting then, he was exiled, living mostly in Iraq, where Iranians largely forgot him until 1978.

A shadowy past followed Khomeini. The 1960s rioting linked to him was financed, in part, by Eastern Bloc intelligence services. He was in the circle of the cleric Kachani Sayed Abolghassem, who had ties to East German intelligence. Furthermore, in 1960, Colonel Michael Goliniewski, second-in-command of Soviet counter-intelligence in Poland, defected to the West. His debriefings exposed so many communist agents that he was honored by a resolution of the U.S. House of Representatives. One report, declassified in 2000, revealed, "Ayatollah Khomeini was one of Moscow's five sources of intelligence at the heart of the Shiite hierarchy."

Nevertheless, as French journalist Dominique Lorenz reported, the Americans, "having picked Khomeini to overthrow the Shah, had to get him out of Iraq, clothe him with respectability and set him up in Paris, a succession of events, which could not have occurred, if the leadership in France had been against it."

In 1978, Khomeini, in Iraq since 1965, was permitted to reside at Neauphle-le-Château in France. Two French police squads, along with Algerians and Palestinians, protected him. Nahavandi notes:

Around the small villa occupied by Khomeini, the agents of many of the world's secret services were gathered as thickly as the autumn leaves. The CIA, the MI6, the KGB and the SDECE were all there. The CIA had even rented the house next door. According to most of the published witness-statements, the East Germans were in charge of most of the radio-transmissions; and, on at least one occasion, eight thousand cassettes of the Ayatollah's speeches were sent, directly to Teheran, by diplomatic bag.

Foreign-affairs analyst du Berrier reported:

French services quickly verified that Libya, Iraq and Russia were providing money. Young Iranians, members of the Tudeh (communist) Party, made up Khomeini's secretariat in France. Working in cooperation with the French Communist Party they provided couriers to pass his orders and tapes into Iran. Their sympathizers in Britain turned the BBC (British Broadcasting Corporation) into a propaganda organ.

Journalists descended in droves on Neauphle-le-Château; Khomeini gave 132 interviews in 112 days, receiving easy questions as their media organs became his sounding board. Nahavandi affirms that, within Iran "the Voice of America, the Voice of Israel and, especially, the BBC virtually became the voice of the revolution, moving from criticism, to overt incitement of revolt, and from biased reporting, to outright disinformation."

Khomeini's inflammatory speeches were broadcast; revolutionary songs aired on Iranian radio. One journalist, however, stunned Khomeini by bucking the trend: intelligence expert Pierre de Villemarest, hero of the French Resistance in World War II, anti-communist, and critic of the CFR. Interviewing Khomeini, de Villemarest asked:

How are you going to solve the economic crisis into which you have plunged the country through your agitation of these past few weeks?... And aren't you afraid that when the present regime is destroyed you will be outpaced by a party as tightly-knit and well organized as the [communist] Tudeh?

Khomeini didn't reply. The interpreter stood, saying, "The Ayatollah is tired." De Villemarest registered his concern with the French Ministry of the Interior, but reported, "They told me to occupy myself with something else."

Ending the Shah's Rule

Iran's situation deteriorated. As Western media spurred revolutionaries, riots and strikes paralyzed Iran. The Shah wrote:

At about this time, a new CIA chief was stationed in Teheran. He had been transferred to Iran from a post in Tokyo with no previous experience in Iranian affairs. Why did the U.S. install a man totally ignorant of my country in the midst of such a crisis? I was astonished by the insignificance of the reports he gave me. At one point we spoke of liberalization and I saw a smile spread across his face.

The Carter administration's continuous demand upon the Shah: liberalize. On October 26, 1978, he freed 1,500 prisoners, but increased rioting followed. The Shah commented that "the more I liberalized, the worse the situation in Iran became. Every initiative I took was seen as proof of my own weakness and that of my government." Revolutionaries equated liberalization with appeasement. "My greatest mistake," the Shah recalled, "was in listening to the Americans on matters concerning the internal affairs of my kingdom."

Iran's last hope: its well-trained military could still restore order. The Carter administration realized this. Du Berrier noted: "Air Force General Robert Huyser, deputy commander of U.S. forces in Europe, was sent to pressure Iran's generals into giving in without a fight." "Huyser directly threatened the military with a break in diplomatic relations and a cutoff of arms if they moved to support their monarch."

"It was therefore necessary," the Shah wrote, "to neutralize the Iranian army. It was clearly for this reason that General Huyser had come to Teheran."

Huyser only paid the Shah a cursory visit, but had three meetings with Iran's revolutionary leaders—one lasting 10 hours. Huyser, of course, had no authority to interfere with a foreign nation's sovereign affairs.

Prior to execution later by Khomeini, General Amir Hossein Rabbi, commander-in-chief of the Iranian Air Force, stated: "General Huyser threw the Shah out of the country like a dead mouse."

U.S. officials pressed the Shah to leave Iran. He reflected:

You cannot imagine the pressure the Americans were putting on me, and in the end it became an order.... How could I stay when the Americans had sent a general, Huyser, to force me out? How could I stand alone against Henry Precht [the State Department Director for Iran] and the entire State Department?

He finally accepted exile, clinging to the belief that America was still Iran's ally, and that leaving would avert greater bloodshed. These hopes proved illusions.

A factor in the Shah's decision to depart was that—unknown to most people—he had cancer. U.S. Ambassador William Sullivan (CFR) assured the Shah that, if he exited Iran, America would welcome him. Despite the pleadings of myriad Iranians to stay, he reluctantly left. However, shortly after reaching Cairo, the U.S. ambassador to Egypt effectively informed him that "the government of the United States regrets that it cannot welcome the Shah to American territory."

The betrayed ruler now became "a man without a country."

Iran's Chaotic Descent

On February 1, 1979, with U.S. officials joining the welcoming committee, Ayatollah Khomeini arrived in Iran amid media fanfare. Although counter-demonstrations, some numbering up to 300,000 people, erupted in Iran, the Western press barely mentioned them.

Khomeini had taken power, not by a constitutional process, but violent revolution that ultimately claimed hundreds of thousands of lives. Numerous of his opponents were executed, usually without due process, and often after brutal torture. Teheran's police officers—loyal to the Shah—were slaughtered. At least 1,200 Imperial Army officers, who had been instructed by General Huyser not to resist the revolution, were put to death. Before dying, many exclaimed, "God save the King!" "On February 17," reported du Berrier, "General Huyser faced the first photos of the murdered leaders whose hands he had tied and read the descriptions of their mutilations." At the year's end, the military emasculated and no longer a threat, the Soviet Union invaded Afghanistan. More Iranians were killed during Khomeini's first month in power than in the Shah's 37-year reign. Yet Carter, Ted Kennedy, and the Western media, who had brayed so long about the Shah's alleged "human rights" violations, said nothing. Mass executions and torture elicited no protests. Seeing his country thus destroyed, the exiled Shah raged to an adviser: "Where are the defenders of human rights and democracy now?" Later, the Shah wrote that there was

> *not a word of protest from American human rights advocates who had been so vocal in denouncing my "tyrannical" regime! It was a sad commentary, I reflected, that the United States, and indeed most Western countries, had adopted a double standard for international morality: anything Marxist, no matter how bloody and base, is acceptable.*

Exile

The Shah's personal tragedy wasn't over. He stayed briefly in Egypt and Morocco, but did not wish to impose risks on his hosts from Muslim extremists. Eventually he welcomed Mexican President Lopes Portillo's hospitality.

However, in Mexico the Shah received an invitation from CFR Chairman David Rockefeller, who used influence to secure permission for the Shah to come to America for medical treatment. Rockefeller sent a trendy Park Avenue MD to examine the Shah, who agreed—against his better judgment—to abandon his personal physicians and fly to New York for treatment. In October 1979, he was received at the Rockefeller-founded Sloan-Kettering Memorial Hospital for cancer treatment. Here the Shah experienced a fateful delay in spleen surgery that some believe accelerated his death.

The Shah's admission to the United States had another outcome. Partly in retribution, on November 4, 1979, Iranians took 52 hostages from the U.S. embassy in Teheran. (According to Nahavandi, Soviet special services assisted them.) This embarrassed Jimmy Carter, who had done so much to destroy the Shah and support Khomeini. The seizure made the Shah a pawn.

While in New York, Mexico inexplicably reversed its welcome, informing the Shah that his return would contravene Mexico's "vital interests." One can only guess at the hidden hands possibly influencing this decision.

Carter faced a dilemma. Iran wanted the Shah's return—for a degrading execution—in exchange for the American hostages. However, a direct trade might humiliate the United States.

Therefore, Panama was selected as intermediary. Following treatment in New York, the Shah was informed he could no longer remain in America, but Panama would welcome him. In Panama, however, the Shah and Empress were under virtual house arrest; it was apparent that it would only be a matter of time before the Shah would be sent to Iran in exchange for the hostages. A special cage was erected in Teheran. Khomeini's followers envisioned parading him in the streets before final torture and bloody execution.

However, Anwar Sadat, the Egyptian president and the Shah's friend, discerned the scheme, and sent a jet to Panama, which escorted the Shah and Empress safely to Egypt.

Mohammad Reza Pahlavi died on July 27, 1980. His last words: "I wait upon Fate, never ceasing to pray for Iran, and for my people.

I think only of their suffering." In Cairo, a grand funeral honored him. Three million Egyptians followed the procession.

Anwar Sadat who, like the Shah, advocated a peaceful Middle East, and defied the American establishment by saving the Shah from infamous death, did not survive much longer himself. The following year, Muslim extremists assassinated him under circumstances remaining controversial.

The Issues

Why did the American establishment, defying logic and morality, betray our ally the Shah? Only the perpetrators can answer the question, but a few possibilities should be considered.

Iran ranks second in the world in oil and natural-gas reserves. Energy is critical to world domination, and major oil companies, such as Exxon and British Petroleum, have long exerted behind-the-scenes influence on national policies.

The major oil companies had for years dictated Iranian oil commerce, but the Shah explained:

> *In 1973 we succeeded in putting a stop, irrevocably, to sixty years of foreign exploitation of Iranian oil-resources.... In 1974, Iran at last took over the management of the entire oil-industry, including the refineries at Abadan and so on.... I am quite convinced that it was from this moment that some very powerful, international interests identified, within Iran, the collusive elements, which they could use to encompass my downfall.*

Does this explain the sudden attitude change toward Iran expressed by Henry Kissinger, beginning in the mid-seventies? Kissinger's links to the Rockefellers, whose fortune derived primarily from oil, bolsters the Shah's view on the situation. However, other factors should be considered.

Although the Shah maintained a neutral stance toward Israel, during the 1973 Yom Kippur War, he allowed critical supplies to reach Egypt, enabling it to achieve a balance of success, and earning Sadat's undying gratitude, but wrath from influential Zionists. Did this impact the West's attitude change in the mid-seventies?

We should not overlook that the Shah opposed the powerful opium trade, now flourishing in the Middle East.

Finally, the Shah was a nationalist who brought his country to the brink of greatness and encouraged Middle East peace. These qualities are anathema to those seeking global governance, for strong nations resist membership in world bodies, and war has long been a destabilizing catalyst essential to what globalists call "the new world order."

What is the solution to modern Iran? Before listening to war drums, let us remember:

It was the CFR clique—the same establishment entrenched in the Bush and Obama administrations—that ousted the Shah, resulting in today's Iran. That establishment also chanted for the six-year-old Iraq War over alleged weapons of mass destruction never found. Therefore, instead of contemplating war with Iran, a nation four times Iraq's size, let us demand that America shed its CFR hierarchy and their interventionist policy that has wrought decades of misery, and adopt a policy of avoiding foreign entanglements, and of minding our own business in international affairs.

The Accusation Donald Trump Did Get Right

Brian Glyn Williams

The following viewpoint by Islamic history professor Brian Glyn Williams posits that Republicans, particularly those involved in the Bush administration, should admit their mistakes in allowing a false claim about weapons of mass destruction to motivate an invasion of Iraq, which caused thousands of deaths and fomented greater instability and violence throughout the Middle East. Williams, who teaches at the University of Massachusetts-Dartmouth, is also the author of scholarly books about American military experiences in Afghanistan, Iraq, and Syria.

Recently Donald Trump broke with the Republican convention and roiled the party base by boldly stating "You call it whatever you want. I want to tell you. They [the Bush administration] lied. They said there were weapons of mass destruction [in Iraq]; there were none. And they knew there were none. There were no weapons of mass destruction." He also stated "We spent $2 trillion, thousands of lives. Obviously, it was a mistake. George Bush made a mistake. We can make mistakes. But that one was a beauty. We should have never been in Iraq. We have destabilized the Middle East."

This typically brash Trump statement went against an unwritten rule in the Republican establishment which states that it is taboo to bring up the subject of the WMDs that were not found after the invasion and occupation of secular-Baathist Iraq (all of the strands of intelligence, from Iraqi killer drones to mobile weapons labs to

---

"At Least Trump Got One Thing Right. There Were No WMDs In Iraq," by Brian Glyn Williams, TheHuffingtonPost.com, April 5, 2016. Reprinted by Permission.

nuclear centrifuges fell apart after the occupation of the country and "exploitation" of its bases and facilities).

If you go to Google "images" and try finding online pictures of U.S. reconnaissance and exploitation troops uncovering the much-hyped Iraqi WMDs—like killer drones that were said to be able to strike American mainland or mobile weapons labs— there are none available. All that was found by the U.S. Army Joint Captured Material Exploitation Group teams were some old, corroded, un-useable, "demilitarized" artillery shells rotting in the desert from the 1980s, a far cry from the active, threatening chemical, biological and even nuclear(!) WMD program we were repeatedly told by Bush, Cheney, Powell, Rice and Rumsfeld that Iraq possessed.

Trump was of course absolutely correct in his bold, in your face statement. But try telling that to the average Republican voter, the majority of whom (63 percent according to a Dartmouth College poll) believe that WMDs were found in Iraq.

It seems the Republican base has a hard time accepting the fact that their president led them into a disastrous war that took the lives of almost 4,500 brave American men and women who thought they were defending their country from WMDs (i.e. fifty percent more than were killed by Al Qaeda on 9/11) and cost three trillion dollars and spawned ISIS (where there had previously been a secular Baathist government with no WMDs) based on cooked up intel.

But the very leaders who sold them the goods on Iraq's non-existent weapons program have (with the exception of Cheney) come out and acknowledged that there were no WMDs. Bush, like Powell before him, ultimately acknowledged that the search for WMDs had ended in failure as reported in his own memoir Decision Points. Bush wrote, "No one was more shocked and angry than I was when we didn't find the weapons. I had a sickening feeling every time I thought about it. I still do." When discussing the lack of WMDs, Bush would later state, "It is true that much of the intelligence turned out to be wrong." In an interview with

5 Reasons the Iraq War Was Not a Mistake

[...]

1. In a post-9/11 world, uncertainty about WMD is not an option.

The central preoccupation of policymakers after 9/11 was preventing any further mass terror attacks against the United States. The George W. Bush administration would have been blamed—and rightly so—if Iraq had used WMD or passed WMD to terrorists. It was not a chance the U.S.—or the world—could afford to take. And given the refusal of Saddam Hussein to cooperate with the UN, there was no alternative.

2. An American force in the Middle East would increase pressure on Iran.

Removing Saddam Hussein meant removing a threat to the Iranian regime. But putting hundreds of thousands of American troops on Iran's western border—along with those already in Afghanistan to the east—meant posing a much more potent threat to the regime. That is why Iran temporarily slowed its nuclear program after 2003—and why the Iranian people found the courage to rise in 2009.

3. Freeing the people of Iraq was, and is, a worthy goal.

Just a few years ago, with American and allied troops still in Iraq in significant numbers, the sectarian violence and terrorism that had plagued the country for years had begun to slow down. The Iraqi people began to enjoy some semblance of order, of democracy, and of liberty. Instead of staying in Iraq to guide and protect that process—as Obama had promised to do in 2008—Obama abandoned the Iraqi people.

4. International law means nothing unless it is backed up by the will to enforce it.

Saddam Hussein defied international law repeatedly: He used WMD against his own people; he invaded his neighbors; he sponsored terrorism. And he did it because he had no fear of facing the consequences. International law, flawed though it is, is a necessary and stabilizing institution—and needs enforcement, even (especially) when global institutions are too corrupt to enforce it.

5. There is potential for freedom in the region–with American leadership.

fall of Saddam Hussein inspired the Lebanese people to rise up against Syrian occupation, and planted the seeds of what later became the Arab Spring. If American leadership had remained strong, that process might have been a positive one. (Certainly Syria would not have become a killing field.) The Middle East may never be fertile soil for democracy, but it can certainly be freer than it is today.

[...]

— "5 Reasons the Iraq War Was Not a Mistake", by Joel B. Pollak,
Breitbart, May 19, 2015

ABC's Martha Raddatz, Bush would once again confirm the lack of WMDs in Iraq:

> Raddatz: Just let me go back because you brought this up. You said Saddam Hussein posed a threat in the post-9/11 world. They didn't find weapons of mass destruction.
> Bush: That's true. Everybody thought they had them.

On yet another occasion, Bush said "Now, look, I didn't—part of the reason we went into Iraq was—the main reason we went into Iraq at the time was we thought he had weapons of mass destruction. It turns out he didn't, but he had the capacity to make weapons of mass destruction."

Secretary of Defense Rumsfeld, who made numerous declarations on the existence of chemical, biological and nuclear weapons in Iraq, also acknowledged making at least one "misstatement" about WMDs. He then stated, "It appears that there were not weapons of mass destruction there." When asked by the BBC about the lack of WMDs in Iraq, Rumsfeld would later say, "Why the intelligence proved wrong, I'm not in a position to say."

In his memoir, *Known and Unknown*, Rumsfeld specifically mentioned the lack of WMD stockpiles in Iraq and said "Saddam Hussein didn't have ready stockpiles of WMD our intelligence community believed we would uncover. The shift in emphasis suggested that Iraq's intentions and capability for building WMD had somehow not been threatening. Many Americans and others around the world accordingly came to believe the war was unnecessary." (page 712)

National Security Advisor Condoleezza Rice similarly acknowledged, "What we have is evidence that there are differences between what we knew going in and what we found on the ground." Secretary of State Colin Powell would also state, "Of course I regret that a lot of it [the evidence] turned out be wrong."

To compound matters, the Iraq Survey Group (ISG) created by President Bush to scour post-invasion Iraq and find hidden WMDs ultimately reported the following definitive findings to the U.S. government once their search was complete:

"Saddam Hussein ended the nuclear program in 1991 following the Gulf war. ISG found no evidence to suggest concerted efforts to restart the program."

"In practical terms, with the destruction of the Al Hakam facility, Iraq abandoned its ambition to obtain advanced BW [biological warfare] weapons quickly. ISG found no direct evidence that Iraq, after 1996, had plans for a new BW program or was conducting BW-specific work for military purposes."

"While a small number of old, abandoned chemical munitions have been discovered, ISG judges that Iraq unilaterally destroyed its undeclared chemical weapons stockpile in 1991. There are no credible indications that Baghdad resumed production of chemical munitions thereafter."

What does all of this mean for the majority of Republicans who still cling to the stated rationale/pretext for invading and dismantling Baathist-Socialist Iraq? It would seem to indicate that they have been grasping onto straws and they should, like the Democrats who previously acknowledged that President Bill Clinton lied to them about the Lewinsky affair, acknowledge the truth, just as the very leaders who deceived them in the first place have belatedly done.

Only a Well-Intentioned Putin Can Help the Peace Process

Luigi Narbone

In the following viewpoint, Luigi Narbone, who serves as the director of the Middle East Directions Programme for the Robert Schuman Centre for Advanced Studies at the European University Institute, questions the intentions of Russian leader Vladimir Putin and his involvement in Syria. Narbone fears that Russian motivation is to gain political power in the region rather than to rid the country of ISIS. Narbone is well-versed in Russian politics. He served on the European Commission delegation in the Russian Federation. Narbone also held key European Union positions as an ambassador in many Middle Eastern countries.

Can Russia succeed where the West has failed, stabilising the Middle East and North Africa through some kind of Pax Russica?

The question might have sounded strange not so long ago, but in less than two years, a mix of decisive action, unwavering and often ruthless use of military power, and bold political-diplomatic manoeuvring have given Moscow new prominence on the global stage.

Russia has managed to regain, at least in part, its role as a powerful interlocutor, which it lost after the fall of the Soviet Union.

In the process, it has fostered relationships with key countries in the region and closed lucrative arms sales deals.

"A Pax Russica in the Middle East? Putin will have to do more to make it stick," by Luigi Narbone, The Conversation, 02/24/2017.

A new Russian-Iranian axis in Syria

In Syria, Russia's air support to President Bashar al-Assad's forces has rescued the regime from likely collapse.

It has dramatically changed the balance of power between forces on the ground, permitting a series of military advances epitomised by the regime's reconquest of Aleppo in December 2016. The moderate opposition has been destroyed in the process.

Russia's direct intervention, which has entailed joining forces with Iran and its proxy Hezbollah, which provides support to Assad's forces on the ground, has led to an ongoing realignment of the regional powers involved in the conflict.

The Gulf countries have disengaged and Turkey has dropped its demand for Assad to go in order to align with the new Russian-Iranian axis.

While the three countries certainly pursue diverging strategic objectives, this alliance of convenience has put them in the driver's seat for the future of the conflict.

Ceasefire and uncertainties

After the fall of Aleppo, Russia, along with Turkey and to a lesser extent Iran, has intensified its diplomatic efforts to broker a cessation of hostilities between warring parties.

Together with Turkey, Russia sponsored the Astana Conference in January.

Invitations to this meeting reflected the new balance of forces after the Aleppo battle, as shown by the choice of non-jihadist military actors called to the talks with the regime's representatives.

While no face-to-face negotiations took place, the warring sides have pledged to consolidate the ceasefire and to resume a political process in Geneva, which is due to start on February 23.

This will necessarily be based on Russia's views about Syria's future. The US, already passive on Syria, and the EU, incapable of playing a military role, have been mere bystanders.

Russia may indeed want to end the conflict and contribute to stabilising Syria, as this would help it to solidify strategic gains in the country and beyond. Yet, many uncertainties stand in the way.

The Astana Conference deepened the divisions between rebel armed groups in Syria, which may well lead to some of them being radicalised further.

Russia is facing difficulties in keeping the Assad forces and Hezbollah in check, as the continuing ceasefire violations show.

Besides, the long-term durability of the troika, formed with Turkey and Iran, may soon be put to the test, especially with wild card Donald Trump in the White House. Ankara is nervous about Moscow's plans regarding Kurdish autonomy in Syria after the war, and had a lukewarm reaction to Trump's proposal to establish safe zones.

Russia and Iran continue to have strategic and tactical differences. Tensions between Iran and the new US administration are already on the rise. Should the predicted US-Russia rapprochement materialise, how long would the Russia-Iran entente last?

Russian investment in the region

Russia's activism has also begun to pay dividends in Libya. Russia chose to put its weight behind the Egypt-aligned general Khalifa Haftar, who leads the Libyan National Army (LNA), providing much advertised economic and military support.

Moscow's backing has allowed Haftar to consolidate his position as an indispensable party into any workable political agreement. But it has also been a way for Moscow to increase its profile as a power-broker in the Libyan stalemate.

Such investment may have important returns in terms of political influence, geo-strategic and economic gains if Libya stabilises.

But Moscow's efforts have not been limited to countries at war. Its relationship with Egypt has been strengthened by Putin's unconditional support towards Egyptian President Abdel Fattah al-Sisi.

With Israel, Russia has tried to underline common interests and reinforce the existing partnership. Despite the major tensions that occurred in 2011-2015, especially over Syria, Moscow is now privileging pragmatic exchanges even with Saudi Arabia and Qatar. This has yielded some results, as shown by the agreement on oil production cuts.

The image of a strong Russia

Moscow had set objectives and, so far, seems to have achieved them. In the face of poor economic performance and perceived Western confrontation in Ukraine and "the near abroad," President Putin needed to counter political discontent at home.

His comeback in the Middle East and the North African region has helped him galvanise popular support for the diehard image of a strong, nationalist Russia that is capable of projecting its power.

Russia has managed to take advantage of the post-2011 chaos and transform it into opportunity.

It has expanded its naval base in Tartus, its only one in the Mediterranean Sea. It has also expanded its influence in the broader Middle East, and set the basis of what could become a new security order in the region.

This has largely been inspired by the objective to fight radicalisation and jihadism at Russia's borders, as well as among its large Muslim populations in southern regions.

So far, Moscow's policy has mostly been based on supporting strongmen, making deals with authoritarian countries, defending existing state structures and borders and striving to recreate stability and a (favourable) regional order.

However, despite the apparent successes that it has produced in the short run, it is unlikely to truly stabilise the region in the long term.

Russia lacks the economic means and the political will required to reach sustainable conflict resolution and durable stabilisation.

Russia also needs dialogue with the West to address the complexities of the MENA region and EU contribution to fund post-conflict reconstruction. However, increasing deterioration of relationships and the growing negative perception of Russia in Western capitals raise serious doubts about the viability of such cooperation.

If it does not tackle the root causes of violence and instability—like the weakening of states and their incapacity to ensure political inclusion, services, security and development to their citizens or the sectarianisation of political conflicts—any attempt to stabilise the region is doomed to fail in the long run.

Left unaddressed, these issues will inevitably cause new crises, making the idea of a Pax Russica illusory.

VIEWPOINTS ON
MODERN WORLD HISTORY

CHAPTER 2

The Major Issues

Preface

Various initiatives over the decades since the establishment of the state of Israel have raised hopes that a stable peace can be brought to the Middle East. But each small triumph, such as the Camp David Accords spearheaded by President Jimmy Carter in 1979, has been overtaken by regression in the peace process. Every step forward is followed by two steps back. The result has often been chaos.

It seems there are too many hot spots to cool down. Whether it is the conflict between Israel and the Palestinians, the ongoing battles between Iran and Iraq, ideological and religious confrontations between various factions, or unabated terrorism meted out by extremists, any realistic pursuits of a sustained peace remains little more than a faraway dream. Even finding enough common ground to lure the combatants to a bargaining table has proven impossible in most cases.

Though the powers-that-be cannot dismiss the past in seeking a better future, those that seek a lasting peace must deal with the present. They must also contend with those whose goal is to create violence and instability. The voices of reason must be stronger than the actions of the terrorists and religious zealots. Those that seek to create peace in the Middle East, even through military means, must prove more effective than those pushing from the other side with their extremism, bombings, and executions. And they must also replace the mindset of those too intolerant to accept others in the region with a new "live and let live" mentality.

Legitimate arguments have been expressed on both sides of each issue. For instance, it has been stated that a lasting peace between Israel and the Palestinians will be impossible unless the former recognizes the latter as an independent state. But, on the other hand, others contend that Palestinians have no intention of living side-by-side with Israel. And neither do other Middle Eastern countries, particularly Iran.

It has also been claimed that only the elimination of religious-based governments and laws can bring stability and peace to the region. But others say that any peace initiatives must find success within that framework because theocracies and dictatorships cannot be toppled without violence. And though it has been stated that terrorism can be stopped through education and raising the quality of life for all people in the Middle East, detractors insist that only crushing terrorists militarily can bring peace.

The answer, to borrow a line from arguably a more hopeful generation, is blowing in the wind. It remains as elusive, perhaps even more so, than ever.

No Recognition of State, No State of Peace

Middle East Eye

American foreign policy changed greatly during the Obama administration, leading Secretary of State John Kerry to proclaim that peace between Israel and other Middle Eastern countries would be impossible if the former did not accept the right of the Palestinian state to exist. That news was reported in the following viewpoint by Middle East Eye, which publishes region-specific columns, features, and essays. The official US policy has since changed—after President Donald Trump took a more hardline pro-Israel stance that did not necessarily include recognition of the Palestinian state.

Peace between Israel and the Arab world is impossible unless Israel accepts the existence of a Palestinian state, US Secretary of State John Kerry said in a major policy speech on Wednesday.

He called the peace process "in jeopardy" and said, "if Israel goes down the one state path, it will never have true peace with the rest of the Arab world".

He also warned that Israeli government policies were seemingly driven by "extreme elements" committed to a single state.

Responding to Danny Danon, the Israeli ambassador to the UN who said that he had expected Washington to back Israel, Kerry said that the US had acted in accordance with its values.

"They fail to recognise that this friend, the United States of America, that has done more to support Israel than any other country, this friend that has blocked countless efforts to

"No peace unless Israel accepts Palestinian State: Kerry," by MEE Staff, Middle East Eye (www.middleeasteye.net), December 29, 2016. Reprinted by permission.

delegitimise Israel, cannot be true to our own values—or even the stated democratic values of Israel—and we cannot properly defend and protect Israel if we allow a viable two-state solution to be destroyed before our own eyes," he said.

"And that's the bottom line: the vote in the United Nations was about preserving the two-state solution. That's what we were standing up for: Israel's future as a Jewish and democratic state, living side by side in peace and security with its neighbours. That's what we are trying to preserve for our sake and for theirs."

Kerry added later: "We reject the criticism that this vote abandons Israel. On the contrary, it is not this resolution that is isolating Israel; it is the permanent policy of settlement construction that risks making peace impossible."

Kerry also criticised the Israeli government of Prime Minister Benjamin Netanyahu, describing his coalition government as the "most right-wing in Israeli history."

Netanyahu had said he was committed to a two-state solution, Kerry said, but his government's agenda appeared geared towards a one-state solution that aimed at creating a "greater Israel."

"This is the most right-wing government in Israeli history with an agenda driven by its most extreme elements," Kerry said.

He also said that the "settlement agenda" was defining Israel, with the proliferation of settlements inadvertently increasing the "security burden" on Israeli forces.

"The settler agenda is defining the future in Israel. And their stated purpose is clear: They believe in one state: greater Israel," he said.

He added that the peace process "goes well beyond settlements."

"Trends indicate a comprehensive effort to take the West Bank land for Israel and prevent any Palestinian development there. Today, the 60 percent of the West Bank known as Area C—much of which was supposed to be transferred to Palestinian control long ago under the Oslo Accords—much of it is effectively off limits to Palestinian development," he said.

"In the end, we could not in good conscience protect the most extreme elements of the settler movement as it tries to destroy the two-state solution. We could not in good conscience turn a blind eye to Palestinian actions that fan hatred and violence. It is not in US interest to help anyone on either side create a unitary state. And we may not be able to stop them, but we cannot be expected to defend them. And it is certainly not the role of any country to vote against its own policies," he said.

Kerry also stated that US policy towards Israeli settlements has not changed for decades, and has been bipartisan.

"It's important to note that every United States administration, Republican and Democratic, has opposed settlements as contrary to the prospects for peace, and action at the UN Security Council is far from unprecedented. In fact, previous administrations of both political parties have allowed resolutions that were critical of Israel to pass, including on settlements."

Friday's resolution was deemed controversial by most of the Israeli political establishment as it was the first time in 40 years a motion condemning Israel had been passed by the UN Security Council where the US traditionally wields its veto on matters relating to it.

It also comes weeks before US president-elect Donald Trump, who is considered an ardent supporter of Israel, is set to take office, replacing incumbent President Barack Obama who has had cool relations with Netanyahu.

Abbas, Netanyahu respond

Following Kerry's speech, Palestinian Authority President Mahmoud Abbas released a statement, saying that Palestine will work with Israel "the minute the Israeli government agrees to cease all settlement activities."

"The Palestinian leadership stands ready to resume permanent status negotiations on the basis of international law and relevant international legality resolutions, including UNSC 2334, under a specified timeframe," it read.

Earlier on Wednesday, Trump said that Israel was being treated "with total disdain and disrespect" and urged it to "stay strong."

> Donald J. Trump (@realDonaldTrump)
> "We cannot continue to let Israel be treated with such total disdain and disrespect. They used to have a great friend in the U.S., but........" 9:19am-28 Dec 2016

> Donald J. Trump (@realDonaldTrump)
> "not anymore. The beginning of the end was the horrible Iran deal, and now this (U.N.)! Stay strong Israel, January 20th is fast approaching!" 9:25am-28 Dec 2016

Netanyahu pushed back against Kerry's statements on Tuesday, saying "Secretary Kerry paid lip service to the unremitting campaign of terrorism that has been waged by the Palestinians against the Jewish state for nearly a century."

"What he did was to spend most of his speech blaming Israel for the lack of peace, by passionately condemning a policy of enabling Jews to live in their historic homeland and in their eternal capital Jerusalem," he added.

He also welcomed Trump's comments in a tweet and said that Israel plans to give him evidence that the US deliberately pushed the Security Council resolution.

> Benjamin Netanyahu (@netanyahu)
> "President-elect Trump, thank you for your warm friendship and clear-cut support for Israel!" 10:24am- 28 Dec 2016

Kerry said that Obama's administration had been "Israel's greatest friend and supporter with an unwavering commitment to protecting its security and legitimacy."

"We have consistently defended the right of Israel to defend itself by itself," he said, condemning Palestinian support for militant groups that threatened Israel.

Kerry said that the buildup of arms by Hamas in Gaza and militant activities there had to stop.

"We have called for the Palestinians to do everything in their power to stop violence and incitement, including publicly and consistently condemning acts of terrorism and stopping the glorification of violence," he said.

"And we have called on them to continue efforts to strengthen their own institutions and to improve governance, transparency, and accountability."

But Kerry also described the plight of 2.75 million Palestinians living "under military occupation" in the West Bank.

"They are restricted in their daily movements by a web of checkpoints so if there is only one state you would have millions of Palestinians living in segregated enclaves under a permanent military occupation that deprives them of the most basic freedoms," he said. "Would an Israeli accept that? Would an American accept that? Would the world accept that?"

Kerry's remarks came as Israel approved the latest batch of settlements being built in the occupied West Bank in defiance of the UN security council resolution that was passed last week.

Following the resolution's passing, Israel suspended diplomatic ties with nations that voted for it.

UN Secretary-General: How About a Little Give-and-Take?

Ban Ki-moon

Secretary-General Ban Ki-moon spoke to the United Nations Security Council in 2016 and urged both sides of the Israel-Palestine conflict to find common ground through compromise in a stronger attempt to reach a peaceful resolution. In the following viewpoint, the UN official, who had recently returned from visits to Israel and Palestine, talked to the Security Council as the fiftieth year of Israeli occupation approached. Among his recommendations was for Israel to allow for greater Palestinian authority in the West Bank. Another was for the Palestinians to condemn attacks against Israelis and to work toward curbing violence.

Following are UN Secretary-General Ban Ki-moon's remarks to the Security Council meeting on the situation in the Middle East, in New York today:

Late last month, I returned from my eleventh visit to Israel and Palestine as Secretary-General. As it happened, it was also as Israel's occupation entered its fiftieth year. I carried a clear and consistent message to leaders on both sides: time is running out.

This fact is also at the heart of the report of the Middle East Quartet. I know the United Nations Special Coordinator for the Middle East, Nickolay Mladenov, has fully briefed you.

"Israeli, Palestinian Leaders Must Make 'Necessary Compromises' to End Political Stalemate, Resume Peace Talks, Secretary-General Tells Security Council", by Ban Ki-moon, United Nations, July 12, 2016. Reprinted by Permission.

Some on both sides have criticized the report's content and sought to dismiss its conclusions and recommendations. The report's overriding message, however, is irrefutable. As negative trends grow more frequent, the prospects of a two-State solution grow more distant.

The report's 10 recommendations provide a practical approach to end the political stalemate, resume the transition to greater Palestinian Authority in the West Bank and chart a course to negotiations to resolve all final status issues.

I urge both sides to immediately begin discussions with the Quartet on implementing these recommendations as we all continue to work in coordination with key stakeholders including regional countries and the United Nations Security Council to restore hope in a political solution. The Quartet envoys are now taking steps in that direction.

The parties will have to make the necessary compromises for peace. At the same time, the region and the wider international community must exercise its influence to encourage both sides. French efforts to pursue peace complement these efforts. I welcome their coordination with the Quartet. I also welcome Egyptian efforts, including the recent visit by [the] Egyptian Foreign Minister to Palestine and Israel.

The failure of Israeli and Palestinian leaders to advance peace has created a vacuum. Extremist voices have filled that space. Recent incidents reinforce the mounting risks. Those responsible for recent terror attacks must be held accountable.

However, closures—such as those in Hebron—as well as punitive demolitions and blanket revocations of permits penalize thousands of innocent Palestinians and amount to collective punishment. I am also deeply troubled by shrinking space for civil society in the region and around the world. I am concerned by Israel's passage of the so-called "NGO Transparency Law", which contributes to a climate in which the activities of human rights organizations are increasingly delegitimized.

All the while, Israel's settlement enterprise marches on. Days after the Quartet called on Israel to cease settlement construction and expansion, Israel announced plans to advance building approximately 560 housing units in the West Bank and 240 more in occupied East Jerusalem. This is in flagrant disregard of international law. These actions constitute an undeniable contradiction to Israel's official support for a negotiated two-State solution. I urge Israel to immediately cease and reverse these plans.

We must ask: How can the systematic expansion of settlements, the taking of land for exclusive Israeli use, and the denial of Palestinian development be a response to violence? Such policies will not bring the two-State solution closer to reality. Such policies will not make Israelis safer or more secure.

As many former Israeli military and intelligence officers have clearly stated, these policies will do precisely the opposite. Indeed, every brick added to the edifice of occupation is another taken from Israel's foundation as a majority Jewish and democratic State.

At the same time, those Palestinians who celebrate and encourage attacks against innocents must know that they are not serving the interests of their people or peace. Such acts must be universally condemned and more must be done to counter the incitement that fuels and justifies terror.

During my visit, I also made my fourth trip to Gaza. Militant activity continues, undermining the fragile ceasefire and threatening to provoke another devastating escalation. Despite significant progress, tens of thousands of people are still displaced following the 2014 conflict. Families are forced to live without electricity for 12 to 18 hours per day. Unemployment remains staggering.

Funds to rebuild Gaza remain elusive. I once again urge donors to fulfil their pledges made in Cairo. But, long-term stability and sustainability for Gaza depends on the lifting of the crippling closures and a re-establishment of a single, legitimate Palestinian governing authority based on PLO [Palestine Liberation Organization] principles.

Turning very briefly to the Golan, I would add that the situation remains volatile and continues to undermine the 1974 Disengagement of Forces Agreement between Israel and Syria, jeopardizing the ceasefire between the two countries.

As we focus on Israeli-Palestinian peace, we must take a hard look at where this conflict stands. How much longer can the parties and the international community accept political paralysis? And at what grave price?

I encourage the Security Council to support the efforts of the Quartet to work with the parties, the region and interested stakeholders in advancing peace. The children of Israel and Palestine deserve nothing less.

I will never forget my moving meeting with student leaders at an UNRWA [United Nations Relief and Works Agency for Palestine Refugees in the Near East] school in Gaza on my final day in the region. One 15-year-old boy concluded by saying "harsh restrictions drain away the ambitions of any young person and this is how we see our future—to be killed by the conflict, to be killed by the closure or to be killed by despair."

Surely, we can do better for all the children of Palestine and Israel. Surely, they deserve a horizon of hope. It is time for the parties to take action to build that future.

The international community, including through the recommendations outlined in the Quartet report, remains resolute in its commitment to support the goal of a peaceful future for both Palestinians and Israelis. That is why I encourage the Security Council to support the efforts of the Quartet—of the United States, the Russian Federation, the European Union and the United Nations—to work with the parties, the region and interested stakeholders in advancing peace.

Peace with Palestinians? Not with Netanyahu

Akiva Elda

A peaceful compromise with the Palestinians has not gained traction since Benjamin Netanyahu became prime minister. He has maintained a hardline, militaristic stance, which was displayed when he brought conservative Avigdor Liberman into the government as minister of defense. In the following viewpoint, Israel Pulse columnist Akiva Eldar asserts that the move will weaken any hopes for initiating peace talks with Palestinians or achieving harmony in that volatile area of the world. Some believe that peace between Israelis and Palestinians can't be accomplished until Netanyahu and his right-wing philosophies have been sidelined.

Any decent people in Israel and around the world are concerned that the decision by Prime Minister Benjamin Netanyahu to bring the right-wing Yisrael Beitenu into the government—rather than the center-left Zionist Camp—and to appoint Yisrael Beitenu leader Avigdor Liberman minister of defense will undermine prospects for a peace process between Israel and the Palestinians. They believe the accusation Zionist Camp leader Isaac Herzog hurled at "radical leftists" in his party for allegedly sabotaging a historic opportunity to promote regional peace. They claim that Netanyahu was a stone's throw from the 2002 Arab Peace Initiative, but as the Americans say, the proof of the pudding is in the eating, and no one is likely to be tasting any of that pudding. On the other hand, Netanyahu has flunked all

"Peace with Palestinians not in Netanyahu's plan," by Akiva Eldar, Al-Monitor, May 24, 2016. Reprinted by Permission.

his previous exams in Regional Peace 101. The grades of deposed Defense Minister Moshe Ya'alon weren't any better.

The current political turmoil will not sabotage prospects for peace. The composition of the new government, like that of its predecessor and the one that never materialized with the Zionist Camp, does not change the fact that zero plus zero equals zero. Even the dovish mien that Netanyahu put on for a brief moment will probably not open the public's eyes to the realization that the king remains a hawk leading them to perdition. For now it would be best to let the United States along with the other members of the Middle East Quartet—the European Union, United Nations and Russia—try their hand at shaking the Israeli public out of its lethargy. All forces of Israeli society, from the enlightened right to the purist left, must be mobilized now to defend democracy.

The first step is to accept that Netanyahu is not going to change. His designated defense minister is not the only one to have honored him with such epithets as "liar" and "crook." The course of history would have been no different had Netanyahu accepted Herzog's demand to personally sign off on the agreements they reached in their talks for a diplomatic initiative. What was Netanyahu's signature worth on the 1998 Wye River Memorandum alongside those of Palestine Liberation Organization Chairman Yasser Arafat and President Bill Clinton? Instead of handing over to the Palestinians parts of Area C in the West Bank, as stipulated by that agreement, Netanyahu transferred (and continues to transfer) the land for the construction of settler homes.

What was the point of Netanyahu's commitment, while a member of the security cabinet of Prime Minister Ariel Sharon, to uproot unauthorized settlement outposts in the West Bank, as laid out in the 2003 road map? Does anyone remember UN Security Council Resolution 1515, unanimously approved at the request of President George W. Bush, to adopt the road map?

A year ago, Netanyahu addressed the lost opportunity to promote a regional peace before a large audience. At a ceremony marking the 70th anniversary of the Allied victory over Nazi Germany, the prime minister explained that interests shared by Israel and the Arab states vis-à-vis Iran were creating opportunities to promote "alliances and possibly move peace forward." So he said, and so what?

Even if Ya'alon not been booted out as defense minister, he would not have salvaged that regional peace approach, in general, nor the two-state solution, in particular. Just a brief reminder: In June 2015 at the Herzliya Conference, Ya'alon had said that he saw no chance of a stable arrangement in the region in his lifetime. Before that, in January 2014, he had said, "The only thing that can 'save' us is for [Secretary of State] John Kerry to win a Nobel Prize and leave us in peace."

I don't know a single political analyst who believes that in Netanyahu's political lifetime, with Herzog and Ya'alon or without them, Israel will move closer to an agreement with the Palestinians. What politician eyeing the country's leadership will offer to give up the occupied territories, knowing that 70% of Jewish Israelis refuse to acknowledge the occupation of the West Bank and East Jerusalem? Beggars can't be choosers, goes the proverb. I can't believe I'm writing this, but for Israelis to keep their state, the slogan "two states for two people" must be archived and replaced by a union of forces to salvage democracy in the State of Israel. The various peace plans must be replaced by a common denominator around which a broad public and alternative leadership can unite— the State of Israel's Declaration of Independence.

Ya'alon, Herzog, left-wing Meretz leader Zehava Gal-On, former Likud Minister Benny Begin, former Likud Minister Gideon Saar, Finance Minister Moshe Kahlon, centrist Yesh Atid leader Yair Lapid, former Likud minister Dan Meridor, Zionist Camp co-leader Tzipi Livni and former Yisrael Beiteinu Knesset member Orly Levy-Abekasis must form a joint political entity and ask the public for a mandate to implement what the fathers of the state envisaged in Israeli's founding document:

No Settlement With Settlements

Palestinian Authority Chairman Mahmoud Abbas said Friday that Israel's continuing settlement activity in the West Bank is preventing a renewal of peace talks.

"We are calling on the international community to intervene on this matter," Abbas told the World Economic Forum meeting in Jordan on Friday.

Abbas underlined the repeated Palestinian call for an independent state with a capital in east Jerusalem.

"We are holding on to a just peace and the two state-solution based on resolutions of international legitimacy, the Arab Peace Initiative and signed agreements, to guarantee an independent Palestinian state with East Jerusalem as its capital," Palestinian news agency Ma'an quoted him as saying.

The Palestinian leader said that Ramallah's efforts to join international forums "is not aimed at any one party" but "is an expression of our desire to build a state according to international standards."

More than 800 leaders from government, business and civil society are attending the two-day event, which hopes to promote growth and development in the region.

—"Abbas: **Israeli settlement activity preventing peace talks**," by JPOST. COM STAFF, Jpost Inc, May 22, 2015.

The State of Israel will … promote the development of the country for the benefit of all its inhabitants; will be based on the precepts of liberty, justice and peace taught by the Hebrew Prophets; will uphold full social and political equality of all its citizens, without distinction of race, creed or sex; will guarantee full freedom of conscience, worship, education and culture. … We yet call upon the Arab inhabitants of the State of Israel to … play their part in the development of the state, with full and equal citizenship and due representation in its bodies and institutions — provisional or permanent.

These principles also guided Theodor Herzl, the visionary of the Jewish state. "My associates and I make no distinctions between one man and another. We do not ask to what race or religion a man belongs. If he is a man, that is enough for us," wrote the father of Zionism in "Altneuland." His moral legacy was "establish your state in such a way that the non-Jew will feel himself well among you."

In "On State and Social Problems," Ze'ev Jabotinsky, the founder of Revisionist Zionism, wrote that of "three evils"—minority rule, anarchy and majority rule—the third is the least evil and thus the preferred choice. The man after whom the headquarters of the Likud movement—the so-called Jabotinsky Fortress—is named wrote that the role of democracy is to ensure minorities a say in running the affairs of state, given that "a minority is but composed of individuals, created in the 'image and likeness of God.'"

There is no certainty that such ruminations would gain Herzl and Jabotinsky entry to the current Knesset. It is fairly certain, however, that if a joint front to salvage democracy in Israel is not soon formed, the legacy of Herzl and Jabotinsky will clear the way for the legacy of the right-wing nationalist Rehavam Zeevi—that is, racism and hatred of the other.

Iran Holds Key to Regional Tranquility

Ehud Yaari

Changes in leadership do not result in a change of motivation in Iran in regard to an expressed desire to destroy Israel, according to Ehud Yaari. The Israel-based Lafer International Fellow of the Washington Institute and Middle East—who is also an analyst on Israeli television—states in this viewpoint that no matter the faction in the Iranian political sphere, one and all seek to wipe Israel off the map. He concludes that Israel must therefore maintain a strong resistance against all Iranian efforts and utilize the aid of the United States to keep its enemy at bay. He asserts that a weaker Iran can provide greater safety for Israel.

The Islamic Republic of Iran has been committed for the past 36 years to a doctrine aimed at wiping Israel off the map. Statements to this effect still pour out of Tehran almost daily. President Hassan Rouhani has somewhat softened his predecessor's language, but does not refrain from expressing his loyalty to this objective. All rival factions within the regime, and many outside too, agree that the destruction of the Jewish State constitutes an important tenet of their devotion to Islam, reflecting a deep ideological conviction in the indispensability of annihilating the "Zionist entity."

Now, some pro-Iranian apologists in the West have claimed that the goal of annihilation does not mandate military means to achieve it, the intimation being that Israel will be destroyed through

"How Iran Plans to Destroy Israel," by Ehud Yaari, The American Interest LLC, August 01, 2015. Reprinted by Permission.

the deployment of truth, faith, and divine power—or through a highly improbable referendum (more on this below). In calling for Israel's demise, Tehran has adopted the line that Israel is an artificial, weak, and split society that will easily implode under pressure—a "spider web" in the words of Hizballah's Secretary General Hassan Nasrallah. At the same time, the Iranians present Israel to their audience as an aggressive, agile opponent that benefits from generous Western support. At the very least, the regime is signaling that a military effort would be essential to bring about a collapse in Israel.

Consequently, much rhetoric is devoted to mobilizing popular support toward achieving this goal. "Death to Israel" is chanted at rallies all across the country, and the mantra is inscribed on a variety of weapons systems in military parades. Supreme Leader Ali Khamenei's mouthpiece, the daily newspaper *Kayhan*, once summed up Iran's stance as follows: "The belief that Israel must be eliminated is a condition of our adherence to Islam. . . . [E]ach and every one of our officials should reiterate our responsibility of the need to destroy this cancerous tumor of Israel." Only some members of the suppressed Green Movement have voiced reservations regarding the regime's prioritization of aiding Israel's adversaries.

Besides demonstrating ideological purity, the disciples of Ayatollah Ruhollah Khomeini see practical benefits in their virulent anti-Israeli posture. Through their repetitive, venomous tirades against Israel they posit Iran as the one true, trustworthy champion of Palestinian rights. The token of this policy has been continuous Iranian support for Palestinian "resistance" movements, the more radical the better. This they contrast with many Arab regimes that seek accommodation with the enemy. Iran thus presents itself as more dedicated to this noble Arab cause than the Arabs themselves. In this way the regime strives to advance Iranian interests by acquiring popularity among Sunni Arabs, thus driving a wedge between the Sunni "street" and its governments.

Yet Iran's policy toward Israel transcends regional posturing and rhetorical ritual. Over the years Tehran's hostile activities support the assessment that Iran is engaged in a sustained campaign to shape the regional landscape for an eventual effort to draw Israel into a doomsday war. This effort started in 1982 with the establishment of Hizballah and evolved into the creation of the Palestinian Islamic Jihad and a military alliance with Hamas. A year ago Iran formed a new militia in Gaza, "al-Sabeerin" (HSN), and more recently it extended itself through attempts to operate proxy groups in Syria along its borders with both Israel and Jordan. Iran has made sure that missiles provided to its partners in the "Axis of Resistance" can reach every coordinate in Israel, and it has invested lavishly in developing and deploying hundreds of long-range missiles capable of hitting Israel from its own territory. These actions testify to the seriousness with which Iran regards its mission.

The Islamic Republic's quest for nuclear weapons offers yet more evidence of its intention to take on Israel at some future date, but not necessarily evidence that it will use these weapons to attack Israel directly. It may be that Tehran seeks a nuclear deterrent to Israeli nuclear weapons, so that the "spider web" can be dispatched without danger to the Iranian homeland. Thus from the Iranian perspective, a nuclear weaponization program is not essential to a final confrontation with Israel. Iranian military strategists seem to think they can eventually destroy the Israeli state without using nuclear weapons.

It is a typical Western liberal conceit to dismiss the threats of autocratic regimes. And it is true that the Iranian regime has proven ready in the past to ignore its declared policies on a variety of issues and change course when politically expedient. Thus, fairly specific threats directed toward the United States, Saudi Arabia, and other actors have been dropped without explanation at different junctures. But its commitment to destroy Israel is a pillar of the Islamic Republic, and so it would seem politically impossible merely to drop it. At the same time, the Iranian regime has consistently refrained from clarifying what role it might play in fulfilling this "religious obligation." Does Iran plan to spearhead, at the appropriate moment, an offensive against Israel? Would Iranian armed forces be directly engaging Israelis on the battlefield? Or would they rather restrict their contribution to arming other combatants and orchestrating their strategy? In short, does the Islamic Republic aspire to become the "liberator" of Jerusalem, or merely a sponsor from afar? Do Iran's leaders envision Arabs celebrating in Palestine, or Iranian troops themselves?

No one knows the answers to these questions, including, very likely, the Iranian leaders themselves. Not everything has gone the mullahs' way, either, in the run-up to achieving their goal. The regime used to have very close relations with Hamas, for example, but the sectarian divisions opened up by the Syrian civil war have introduced great tension into that relationship. Indeed, the deepening of the sectarian divide in recent years has neutered the Iranian attempt to use the Palestine issue to harm Sunni Arab regimes.

Perhaps such perturbations help explain why over the past four decades Iranian leaders have remained ambiguous, never explicitly threatening an assault on Israel at some future date, but never ruling it out either. They have also studiously avoided clashes with the Israeli military, mounting no retaliation for Israeli attacks on ships loaded with Iranian arms in the Red Sea, strikes against storage facilities for Iranian missiles in Syria and Sudan, and even the killing of an Iranian general on the Syrian Golan. They keep stressing the need for "Muslim unity," bringing together rival states for the common purpose of attacking Israel. But they have never gone kinetic directly against it.

Needless to say, the call for Muslim unity is widely understood, including in Israel, to be no more than lip service to an elusive dream. More credible is the Iranian emphasis on the potential role of an effective Palestinian "resistance" that would confront Israel aided by allies such as Hizballah. Still, the Iranians themselves never address the question of whether such a coalition would be capable of defeating the Israel Defense Forces (IDF) on its own.

None other than Iran's favorite proxy, Hizballah Secretary General Nasrallah, referred in April to these unanswered questions in a lengthy interview granted to Syrian official television. "We are not claiming that Hizballah is capable of launching a war", he said.

> *We are incapable of this. Are we expected to lie to the people or to ourselves and say that we are capable of launching a war against Israel and wiping it off the map and liberating Palestine? We have never claimed anything like this.*

Nasrallah also stated that, contrary to previous warnings, he cannot promise that Hizballah fighters could capture any part of the Galilee and certainly "not all the area on the way to Tel Aviv and Eilat." His conclusion was that none of the resistance movements are up to this task, and therefore that a decision to wage a war of this magnitude should be made by "partners who are able to accomplish the goal." He was clearly implying that said partner would be Iran. On the occasion of the recent Qods Day Nasrallah explicitly said that Iran remains "the only threat" to Israel's existence.

Nasrallah's exceptional statement amounts to an open admission that Iran's active participation in a war against Israel would be indispensable, and therefore the decision to launch a war belongs to Tehran. Although overlooked at the time by most Western media, this interview reveals Nasrallah's true calculation of the balance of power in the region; it certainly reflects, as well, Hizballah's significant losses incurred fighting in the Syrian civil war.

The Iranian government has refrained from all official comment on Nasrallah's statement, which was mentioned only briefly in the Farsi press. Iranian authorities, it would seem, were not overly pleased with their protégé's insinuation that, at the end of the day, everything rests in Tehran's hands.

Iran's stated policy, as recently refined by President Rouhani, is to proceed with a strategy of "active deterrence." Upgrading the accuracy of Iranian missiles is, in his view, both "moral and humane" because it can deter Israeli attack. Yet Iranian officials declare repeatedly that the regime has no desire to threaten or attack anybody, or to seek territorial expansion. Iranian analysts occasionally reinforce these proclamations by noting that for two centuries Iran has not initiated a war on any front. Indeed, the last major Iranian military campaign took place on Iranian soil when Reza Shah recaptured the city of Ahwaz, in Khuzestan province, from its rebellious Arab emir, Sheik Khaza'al, in 1925.

With regard to Israel, no record exists of any official military threats beyond the context of retaliation for an Israeli strike on Iran's nuclear installations. The Iranians have simply escalated their warnings in line with their growing confidence that Israel either lacks a credible military option or has become less inclined to employ it. Khamenei himself led this escalation of retaliatory threats, which was invariably echoed by the top brass of the Islamic Revolution Guard Corps (IRGC) and the regular army.

The escalation consisted of four distinct stages. First, Khamenei reacted to the public debate in Israel concerning the wisdom of a preemptive strike on Iran's nuclear installations by declaring that no "hit-and-run" attack against Iran's atomic program was possible. This was interpreted by the Iranian media as indicating "that there could be no possibility that an attack against Iran would go unanswered."

The second stage was Khamenei's adoption in public of a "threat for threat" posture that signaled, according to pro-regime analysts, "that in addition to being ready to thwart all kinds of threats, Iran was actually posing new threats against its enemies." The third step occurred on February 3, 2012, when the Supreme Leader proclaimed, following the Pillar of Defense operation in Gaza, that Iran will help and support anyone prepared to engage the Israelis. One Iranian commentator explained that, "these threats against Iran, having failed to push the Islamic Republic into passivity, have further emboldened it to prepare itself for long term and energetic confrontation with its enemies."

Shortly thereafter, on March 20, during a public address in Mashhad, Khamenei swore explicitly "to raze Tel Aviv and Haifa to the ground" in response to an Israeli strike. The message is clear:

Iran's missiles are on the alert to hit Israel. Other regime spokesmen pointed to the nuclear reactor in Dimona as an additional likely target for instant retaliation.

The threat to Dimona is something of an old story. As early as August 17, 2004, General Mohammed Baqer Zolqadr of the IRGC noted:

> *If Israel fires one missile at the Bushehr atomic power plant, it should permanently forget about its Dimona nuclear center, where it produces and keeps its nuclear weapons, and Israel would be responsible for the terrifying consequences of this move.*

General Yadollah Javani, head of the IRGC's Political Bureau, said such a retaliatory attack would be carried out by "Shehab-3" long-range ballistic missiles. Other Iranian officials mentioned, among other possible targets, Israeli gas fields in the Eastern Mediterranean.

As such statements attest, in order to obtain robust retaliatory capabilities, Iran is relying on its rapidly growing arsenal of long-range missiles. It has also provided tens of thousands of shorter-range rockets and missiles to clients such as Hizballah, Palestinian Islamic Jihad, and Hamas, which could be urged to help respond to an Israeli strike. Iranian officials often take pride in the fact that missiles with ever improving guidance systems stationed in Lebanon—and to a lesser extent in Gaza—can now reach Israel's entire territory.

Iran's missile development in general since 1980 is beyond the scope of this essay; suffice it to say that the leaders have long emphasized to Iranian military commanders the need to develop missiles that can reach Israel in particular. This began with Khamenei's order for missiles with a 1,000-kilometer range that, if launched from Iran's western border, could hit Israel. Still later, Khamenei instructed his commanders to acquire missiles with a 2,000-kilometer range, allowing for a successful hit on Israel from most of Iran's territory. And later still Khamenei personally ordered that the accuracy of the missiles should be dramatically improved. Not surprisingly, therefore, the IRGC's Aerospace Force and Missile Unit commander, Amir Ali Hajizadeh, and his deputy, Majid Mousavi, stated directly that the unit was established in order to attack Israel. Mousavi elaborated last year on the logic of the missile program, saying that, "the Supreme Leader set a particular goal for us based on the assumption that the Zionist regime is our main enemy, and that, if it is decided that we should confront it, missiles with a 2,000-kilometer range would be sufficient."

According to current estimates, Iran deploys approximately 400 missiles capable of hitting Israel. The missile brigades are based in some two dozen locations in central and western Iran. This would allow the Iranians to fire volleys that compound the challenge to Israel's Arrow defense batteries.

Besides their impressive missile arsenal (the largest in the region), the Iranians have so far acquired only limited additional capabilities for engaging Israel directly—other than resorting to terrorist operations. Their aging air force has a poor chance, if any, of reaching Israel. Their new domestically produced ships and submarines would face major difficulties in reaching the Red Sea and Mediterranean but could theoretically attempt to impose, together with the Houthi militias of Yemen, a blockade on Israeli shipping through the Bab al-Mandeb Strait, similar to the blockade imposed there by the Egyptian Navy in 1973. Iran's ground forces for the foreseeable future are unprepared to mount any large-scale multidivisional attack on the distant Israeli frontier, though some elite IRGC units could be sent to Syria to join Hizballah in Lebanon.

Of course, all this may change if Iran decides to allocate resources, derived from the lifting of sanctions and the unfreezing of its financial assets abroad, as a result of a P5+1 nuclear deal, to a major effort to project military power beyond its borders. The S-300 air defense batteries to be supplied from Russia could also greatly improve Iran's defensive posture, while other deals for offensive weapons systems are being considered, or are at least rumored to be. One such deal is the possible purchase of 250 Sukhoi-30 MKM fighters from Russia and/or J-10s from China, and the purchase of dozens of IL-78 MKI aerial tankers. Yet it is obvious that Iran's reliance on its long-range missile arsenal will remain for a long time the backbone of its military strategy with regard to Israel.

As for calls within Iran to take it to Israel offensively, rather than simply prepare to counter an Israeli strike, these have been rare—notably by the now imprisoned former presidential candidate Ahmed Tavakoli—and have received a decidedly cool reception from the regime elite. Instead, that elite, at its very apex, has from time to time spoken in frankly ridiculous terms about how to destroy Israel. The most authoritative, and coldly detached, interpretation of the "death to Israel" slogan came from the Supreme Leader himself in his November 2014 plan titled "9 Key Questions about the Elimination of Israel", posted on his Twitter account. "The proper way of eliminating Israel", he wrote, is through a "public referendum" for all of the "original people of Palestine including Muslims, Christians, and Jews wherever they are." However, the "Jewish immigrants who have been persuaded into emigration to Palestine do not have the right to take part." Following such a referendum, the new government will have to decide if "non-Palestinian emigrants" can remain in the country. Khamenei commented further that destroying Israel does not mean the "slaughter of the Jewish people in the region" but he then went on to call for "arming the people of the West Bank." There was no mention of Iranian involvement in forcing Israel to accept the proposed referendum.

The "arming of the people of the West Bank" had been articulated as a policy shift even before Khamenei's nine-point plan arrived. The logic of this approach requires little explanation. Turning the West Bank into a second Gaza, armed with missiles, trained militias, and controlled by the resistance (Hamas and Islamic Jihad), would create a threat to the heart of Israel. And this, at least, has not been empty talk. Since the outbreak of the Second Intifada in 2000, the IRGC's "Qods Force" has been smuggling money into the West Bank, mainly through Jordan and Turkey, or via Israeli Arabs, and by using exchange bureaus. Both Hizballah and Hamas are trying to enlist West Bank operatives and furnish them with the know-how to manufacture homemade rockets. The importance allocated by Iranian strategists to the West Bank may explain why Tehran does not rule out the establishment of a rump Palestinian state, since IDF withdrawal from it would enhance the prospects of reviving resistance groups there.

The Iranians are likewise investing much effort lately to establish a "resistance" base for operations along parts of the Golan Heights frontier. The goal is to extend the Hizballah-Israeli front in South Lebanon to the Syrian Golan. Though this effort has not been crowned with great success so far, the Iranians seem bent—together with Hizballah—on using Syrian President Bashar al-Assad's dependence on their support to turn southern Syria into a new arena of operation against Israel. Under IRGC commanders, Hizballah is busy recruiting local Druze and others to stir up the Golan frontier by planting IEDs and lobbing occasional mortar shells. Iranian commentator Amir Moussavi summarized this new effort as being aimed at turning the Golan into "a free military area", thus abandoning Assad's traditional objection to heating up the front.

The Iranians' short-term vision thus has Israel squeezed by four fronts of *moqawama* (resistance): Lebanon, southern Syria, Gaza, and, most importantly, the West Bank. Such a scenario would provide them with plenty of opportunities to keep their proxies engaged with Israel, paving the road to a long-term war of attrition masterminded by Tehran and backed by its missile arsenal, with or without nuclear warheads. As Khamenei put it last year, "the only solution is its [Israel's] annihilation and liquidation. Of course, until that moment, the determined and armed Palestinian resistance and its spread to the West Bank are the only way to deal with that bestial regime. . . . [T]herefore, it is my belief that the West Bank should be armed just like Gaza." Affirming this commitment in July 2014, Basij commander Mohammed Reza Naqdi urged all resistance factions to conclude a defense pact against Israel to resurrect the old, pre-Syrian civil war military cooperation agreement between

Hizballah and Hamas and expand it to include other resistance factions. The objective would be to present Israel with the specter of a two- or three-front challenge in any future outbreak of fighting in Gaza or on the Lebanon-Syrian front.

Assuredly, it is no easy task to topple the Palestinian Authority in the West Bank or to achieve freedom to mobilize underground networks and then deliver arms to them. But the Iranians claim that even under the current circumstances they have devised smuggling routes to transfer weapons to the West Bank. Still, so far, security cooperation among Israel, the PA, and Jordan has managed to foil Hamas's attempt to resurrect a military wing in the West Bank. Several attempts to establish workshops for missile production in the West Bank have been uncovered at an early phase.

Iran's idea of besieging Israel with a "resistance wall" constitutes yet another dimension of its thinking. Some Iranians imagine the creation of a land corridor from Iran through Shi'a regions in Iraq to its desert al-Anbar province and from there to Syria and Lebanon. Establishing such a corridor would require at least the tacit cooperation of the authorities in Baghdad (where Iran already enjoys predominance) or the power brokers in Iraq's southern provinces. It would definitely require the Iran-sponsored "Popular Mobilization" units and the various other IRGC-backed Shi'a militias to overcome the Islamic State's current control over key sectors of western Iraq so that it could link up with the Euphrates River Valley in Syria. As yet, the deployment of Shi'a militias into western Iraq has only been tentative, but the issue is under debate. Some militiamen have made it all the way to Damascus to protect that capital from a Sunni onslaught, so anything is possible.

If ISIS loses ground in Anbar and eastern Syria as a result of U.S.-led coalition strikes, and if Damascus remains a member of the "Axis of Resistance," the Iranian corridor to the Israeli frontier could come about in due course, allowing in the more distant future the transport of military supplies and even personnel through the desert to the frontlines. Such a development might even encourage Iranian planners to contemplate launching an expeditionary force in the event of a confrontation.

The Islamic Republic regards its commitment to the destruction of Israel as a long-term project that would require major shifts in the regional political landscape. While displaying a great deal of ambiguity concerning its direct role in a decisive confrontation with Israel, for obvious reasons, Tehran emphasizes its ongoing effort to improve the capability of Palestinian, Lebanese, and Syrian resistance movements to face Israel. The main, immediate target is turning the West Bank into a solid base for military operations. Obviously, the Iranians are well aware that Israel is determined to prevent a takeover of the West Bank by hostile groups. At the same time, they realize that, despite their enormous investment in Hizballah, the group cannot be expected to carry out a "final" war with Israel, especially when it is spending most of its blood and treasure fighting and dying in Syria.

The Iranians are bent on strengthening their influence in the Arab world, with a priority on achieving a land link from Iran to the Mediterranean through Iraq, Syria, and Lebanon. Such a link, once obtained, would allow Iran not only to beef up the resistance movements with Iraqi and Syrian militias, as well as volunteers from far away Afghanistan, but also to open the way to the ultimate introduction of Iranian troops to the lines of confrontation, especially on the Golan. Not for no reason have Iranian generals been strutting around up there lately (and sometimes meeting an untimely demise).

For the United States, which wants to avert an eventual Iran-Israel war, a major priority should be preventing the creation of this land corridor. This will require further efforts to strengthen the government in Baghdad and diminish the power of Iranian-led Shi'a militias operating there. Helping the Iraqi army achieve effective control of Anbar province is likewise crucial. But, as has been shown lately, this is far from easy.

Weakening and ultimately ousting the Assad regime should also remain a top U.S. priority, despite the temptation to discount

Damascus as a threat given the danger of ISIS. Iran's strategic planning would suffer a severe blow if the Assad regime were toppled and Syria no longer served as an ally of Hizballah and a base for Iranian supplies. The recent setbacks suffered by pro-Assad forces present an opportunity to increase military pressure on the regime and its Iranian sponsors. On this count, the most promising sector for a rebel push toward Damascus is southern Syria, where combinations of rebel militias have managed to block the regime's counter-offensive and maintain positions close to the capital's southern outskirts. As Nasrallah himself put it bluntly in May, the fall of Assad and his Iranian allies would mean the "fall of Hizballah, too", since it will be locked into a small enclave within Lebanon.

Naturally, Jordan must be assisted in its efforts to frustrate Iranian activities aimed at undermining the Kingdom and recruiting local Palestinians and east Jordanians along Israel's longest border. Indeed, Jordan's precarious stability would be worsened by Iranian hegemony over neighboring Syria and Iraq. Until now, Tehran has been cautious in its effort to obtain followers and influence in Jordan, but few doubt that Jordan is regarded by Iran as an important potential staging area for future operations against Israel.

Finally, it is absolutely imperative to prevent Iran from acquiring nuclear weapons. Here one need only to recall the infamous statement by ex-president Hashemi Rafsanjani on Qods Day, December 14, 2001:

> *If one day, the Islamic World is also equipped with weapons like those that Israel possesses now, then the imperialists' strategy will reach a standstill because the use of even one nuclear bomb inside Israel will destroy everything. However, it will only harm the Islamic world. It is not irrational to contemplate such an eventuality.*

Such a statement has not been repeated since, given consistent Iranian denials about seeking a nuclear weapon. However, Rafsanjani's declaration evoked Palestinian warnings—including by Hamas leader Khaled Meshal—that Iran should take into account that not only Israelis, but many Palestinians, would die in a nuclear bombing of Israel.

Whatever the risks, nuclear bombs will boost Iran's claim to hegemony in the region and will encourage its leaders to pursue even more aggressive and adventurous policies with respect to Israel. Such policies will be advanced by a coalition of terrorist groups, equipped with thousands of state-of-the-art missiles under a nuclear umbrella. One should assume that if Israel concludes that such a threat is imminent, it will see itself as having no other choice than to undertake a preemptive military strike that would trigger a wide confrontation.

Iran, then, must be kept away from nuclear weapons and at the same time kept as far as possible from Israel's borders, if Washington and its allies wish to avoid a direct Iran-Israel confrontation. Along these lines, a nuclear deal between Iran and the P5+1 might keep Iran from a breakout for a decade or so, but it will at the same time allow Iran to improve its pursuit of different weaponization options, once a decision is made to proceed along those lines.

In the meantime, efforts should be directed at curtailing Iran's drive to broaden the "Resistance Wall" around Israel. This requires not only Israeli measures to insulate the West Bank from Iranian penetration and foil attempts to establish a new front on the Golan Heights, but also a determined U.S.-led effort, together with regional allies, to prevent an Iranian victory in Syria and curb Iranian predominance in Iraq. A direct connection exists between the battle for the Levant and the danger of a war between Iran and Israel. The emergence of an Iran-led "Shi'a crescent", as depicted first by Jordan's King Abdullah, will surely energize the Islamic Republic's oath to destroy Israel.

[Note: After this article went to press, Iran's Supreme Leader Ali Khamenei published a 416-page book with the title "Palestine." His directions on how to proceed toward the destruction of Israel support most of the preceding arguments concerning Tehran's strategy.]

How Should the US Deal with ISIS?

David Coates

Arguments for and against the effectiveness of US air strikes and other potential military action against the terrorist group ISIS abound, according to Wake Forest University professor of Anglo-American Studies David Coates. The following viewpoint details both sides of those arguments. He adds his view of how the military policies in seeking to destroy ISIS have affected US politics. Coates understands the issue fully. He has written extensively on public policy in both the United States and United Kingdom and has authored a book titled Observing Obama in Real Time.

I n an earlier posting, the case was made that what we desperately need in contemporary America is a national conversation about the appropriate direction of our foreign policy, and about the adverse impact on conditions at home of excessive military activity overseas.

As the military campaign against ISIS builds in both Syria and Iraq, that national conversation becomes ever more essential.

There are strong arguments, now widely circulating in the general media, making the case for the persistence (and indeed the intensification) of U.S. airstrikes against ISIS targets. But equally there are strong arguments, less frequently heard perhaps, for why the United States should not continue, and should certainly not intensify, those airstrikes. With public opinion still seriously divided on the issue, though now beginning to slightly drift in

"Weighing the Arguments on U.S. Military Action Against ISIS," by David Coates, TheHuffingtonPost.com, May 9, 2015. Reprinted by Permission.

favor of military action, there is genuine value to be gained by calmly setting the two sets of arguments down together, the better to be able to see their relative strengths and weaknesses. Hence, what follows:

The Case for a Sustained Military Campaign to "Degrade and Ultimately "Destroy" ISIS

So why should the US military be engaged in a sustained air campaign against ISIS strongholds in Syria and Iraq? The official justification for that engagement was the one given by the President in his September address launching the anti-ISIS coalition and announcing limited military action in the Middle East. It was that "if unchecked, these terrorists could pose a growing threat beyond that region - including to the United States. While we have not yet detected specific plotting against our homeland," Barack Obama told his national audience, "ISIL leaders have threatened America and our allies" and "posed a threat to the people of Iraq and Syria, and the broader Middle East—including American citizens, personnel and facilities." Hence our determination "to degrade and ultimately destroy" ISIS.

Behind those generalities stand at least these six specific reasons for military action against the Islamic State.

- *ISIS constitutes a new level of horror.* This threat is not like any other. It is even more barbaric than al Qaeda before it. If unchallenged, its regimen of beheadings, burnings and crucifixions will take us all back into the worst practices of the Middle Ages. As the President put it in that September address: "In a region that has known so much bloodshed, these terrorists are unique in their brutality." Or, to follow Graeme Wood in his recent influential article in The Atlantic: the "fighters of the Islamic State" are "authentic throwbacks to early Islam and are faithfully reproducing its norms of war" (which happen to include "slavery, crucifixion and beheadings.") Something uniquely nasty is afoot in the world - something not really seen since the 1930s and the

Nazis, and something that has already taken American lives in a grotesque way - something that needs to be dealt with effectively and with all due speed.

- *ISIS is determined to build a caliphate. That affects directly the interests of more moderate Arabic forces that are allies of ours. It even threatens non-Arabic countries way beyond its borders.* As Graeme Wood said in that Atlantic article, ISIS "already rules an area larger than the United Kingdom," and if his reporting is right, because it is a caliphate, "It has already taken up what Islamic law refers to as 'offensive jihad,' the forcible expansion into countries that are ruled by non-Muslims." "Following takfiri doctrine," Wood argues, 'the Islamic State is committed to purifying the world by killing vast numbers of people." If true, the parallels with Hitler - which Wood draws - are obvious, and the required response equally unavoidable.

- *So much US effort has gone into building a new Iraq: to see it dissipated so quickly raises questions about why all that sacrifice was necessary; and not fighting on lets down those who fought before.* The United States military lost over 4000 soldiers as casualties of the Iraq war, and sent home at least 32,000 more who were physically and mentally damaged. The wars in Iraq and Afghanistan cost at least $1.26 trillion from start to finish (and the overall "war on terror" maybe $8 trillion): so to see the Iraqi "democracy" that was left behind - not to mention its army - disintegrate so rapidly before the ISIS onslaught, is simply too much for many to bear.

- *The normal "pottery barn rules" apply. We broke it. We own it. We cannot walk away now.* Even those reluctant to admit US culpability in destabilizing pre-2003 Iraq often quietly concede that American intervention is the backdrop to the rise of ISIS, and that in consequence the United States has a particular moral responsibility to somehow stop the rot. At the very least, as the war critic Noam Chomsky had it, defeating ISIS must start "with the US admitting its role in creating this fundamentalist monster." There were even echoes of this argument in the President's September 2014 explanation of why he, of all people, was willing to reconstruct a Bush-like coalition of the willing to engage in extensive military intervention in the Middle East - that while he was adamant that "American forces...will not get dragged into another ground war in Iraq" he was equally clear that American forces were needed there "to support Iraqi and Kurdish forces with training, intelligence and equipment." But why that need, if the United States did not already bear some underlying prior responsibility?

- *ISIS is a global force. We cannot ignore it. We can only resist it.* Appeasement did not work in the 1930s, and it will not work again now. ISIS is not simply focused on Iraq and Syria alone. Instead, "the ISIS cancer has metastasized, as the al Qaeda cancer did before it. The two are now competing to see which can kill more people faster." As the readers of The Wall Street Journal were told in February, ISIS's "often stated objective is to 'remain and expand';" through a complex global strategy "across three geographic rings." "An 'Interior Ring' ...Iraq and...the Levantine states of Syria, Jordan, Lebanon and Israel-Palestine...; the 'Near Broad Ring' that includes the rest of the Middle East and North Africa....; and 'The Far Abroad Ring' that includes the rest of the world, specifically Europe, the U.S. and Asia."

- *ISIS is waging a Holy War against Christendom. Like earlier crusaders, the United States must wage holy war in return.* As Bill O'Reilly told his "Factor" audience in February, echoing the imagery of a clash of crusaders used by the ISIS leadership itself, "the Holy War is here and unfortunately it seems the president will be the last one to acknowledge it." And it is a very serious and dangerous war - one that we must win over there before we lose it over here. Indeed, according to Senator Lindsay Graham at least, "the chance of getting attacked goes up every day." Which is why, as he put it on

Fox News Sunday in September, ""this president needs to rise to the occasion before we all get killed here at home."

The Case for Scaling Back the U.S. Military Campaign Against ISIS

The arguments for scaling back US military involvement in the fight against ISIS call many of the pro-war claims into serious question. The counter-arguments include at least these.

- *We inflate ISIS by attacking it.* ISIS is a regional force. We only make it global by fighting it. As with Al Qaeda before it, a military response by the United States falls directly into the ISIS play book. After 9/11, the United States had little choice but to pursue bin Laden - into Afghanistan at least, if definitely not into Iraq. But with ISIS, where is the immediate threat to US security that makes an all-out war necessary? There is none. As the former head of MI6 told a British audience in the summer of 2014, "the west was not the main target of the radical fundamentalism that created ISIS" since "the conflict was essentially one of Muslim on Muslim." Giving ISIS what he called "the oxygen of publicity" was bound to be counter-productive; and so it is proving. But how could it be otherwise, given what we now know about the self-sustaining nature of an open-ended "war on terrorism." When that war began, there were some 1500 acts of terror recorded throughout the world as a whole. In 2013 there were nearly 10,000. Sixty percent of those remained concentrated in just five countries—in Iraq, Afghanistan, Pakistan, Nigeria and Syria—but did so now in a list that also includes New York, Washington, London, Madrid and Paris. As Christopher Ingraham reported, "After 13 years, 2 wars and trillions in military spending, terrorist attacks are rising sharply." So in such a context, it is worth asking the question. Do we make ourselves more secure by waging air-strikes on an enemy that has goaded us into war, or do we make ourselves less secure?

- *Going to war with ISIS gives terrorists too much influence over American foreign policy.* And we were goaded into this war. ISIS knows that its status is improved in radical Islamic circles if it is attacked by the United States. At a critical moment we may come to regret, we let ISIS's exploitation of social media determine our foreign policy. The execution of American journalists undeniably required a military response: something commensurate to the act. It did not, of itself, require an open-ended commitment to full-scale war. Video of the murder of James Foley was released on August 19, and of Steven Sotloff on September 2nd. The decision to "degrade and ultimately destroy" ISIS in a military campaign that John Kerry conceded "may take a year. It may take two years. It may take three years" came just eight days later. That was way too quick. Joe Biden promised to pursue ISIS to the gates of hell; and when he said that, many of us were equally incensed. But that commitment to a new and prolonged war was made in the heat of a moment of deep national outrage; and once made, could not easily be pulled back. But just because such a commitment was made, it does not mean that it was automatically either right or wise; and in truth, it was neither. The gates of hell are, after all, an extremely long way away, and getting there is going to be extraordinarily costly in both human and financial terms.

- *Do we really want to endure a series of endless wars?* We know about those costs because we have already visited the gates of hell twice since 9/11: first in Afghanistan and then in Iraq. So to attack ISIS in the manner proposed by the President effectively opens up our third Middle Eastern war in less than two decades, and yet another huge military endeavor in what is increasingly proving to be a semi-permanent American condition—namely war itself. Just think of how many wars America has fought since 1945; and ask yourself just how many of those have we actually won? The President's request to Congress does set a three-year limit to the authorization to use military force on this occasion; but it still seeks that authorization, and it cannot by itself guarantee that, once given, the authorization will not also be regularly renewed. Indeed, it seems more likely than not that it will be renewed, because mission creep appears endemic to military engagements of this kind. Even the Afghan war - supposedly entirely over for US forces by 2014 - is now drawing US military personnel back in again. That war was not a success. Nor by any meaningful standards was the invasion of Iraq: so why should this new one be any different? We don't honor our own dead by increasing their number in more futile fighting. And we don't do our existing military personnel any favors by pretending that they could take on another Middle Eastern ground war on their own. If Lindsay Graham wants that ground war, he should be out there arguing for the return of the draft. The fact that he isn't tells us exactly what we know: that talk is cheap in Washington, in a country which ultimately has no stomach for unending military adventurism abroad.

- *This is not our fight alone, nor is it our fight to lead.* The battle with ISIS is primarily a fight between Muslims anchored firmly in an Islamic world. It is in consequence "an ideological war," that, as Fareed Zakaria has properly argued, "America must watch, not fight." If ISIS is to be defeated, that defeat will have to come from other more moderate Arab forces based in the Middle East itself. The King of Jordan, among others, is very clear on that. "This is not a Western fight," he told Zakaria, 'this is a fight inside of Islam where everybody comes together against these outlaws." He wants "international support and involvement, but is wary of Western troops." And well he might be: for when western armies lead the fight, their very presence helps discredit the moderate local forces they are there to support, by allowing them to be presented by their local critics either as tools of American imperialism or as too weak to fight alone, or as both. ISIS knows that. That is presumably why they have worked so hard to provoke an American military response. The former US soldier Emile Simpson got it right in ways that Lindsay Graham so far has not. Drawing on his military experience in Afghanistan, he argued just two days after the Obama address that, "the lessons of the past decade suggest that a clearly bounded extension of US military action means taking responsibility at most for the initial phase, not the permanent defeat of ISIS in which the west should play only a supporting role." And even that role is better orchestrated through existing international institutions rather than through ad hoc coalitions of the willing. NATO is certainly available for that purpose even if the UN Security Council is not.

- *Right now we are locked in a series of contradictions:* fighting a war of choice initiated by a president hitherto keen to reduce America's role in the world; supporting the Saudi's when their modes of punishment are as barbaric as those of ISIS; and condemning Iran when Iran is part of the fight against ISIS. The starkest example of that contradiction occurred on the very day that Israeli Prime Minister Benjamin Netanyahu appeared before the US Congress, implying the need for military action against Iran. Simultaneously, the *Wall Street Journal*—on its front page—reported the beginnings of an Iraqi army offensive against ISIS outside Tikrit. It reported assistance from an outside power, "throwing drones, heavy weaponry and ground forces into the battle." The outside power was not the United States. It was Iran. The grounds forces were Iranian Revolutionary Guards. The major external ally to the United States in the military again against ISIS—the Sunni radicals—is currently, Shiite Iran—the very country that Netanyahu would have us believe is our major enemy in the region! He might be comfortable solving that conundrum by telling members of Congress that "when it comes to Iran and ISIS, the enemy of your enemy is your enemy." But the sounder lesson to be drawn is surely the one we learned the hard way in Iraq after 2003: namely that the trick in Middle Eastern quagmires is not to thrash about or to charge forward. The trick is rather not to enter them in the first place; and if inadvertently already in, then to slowly and carefully step out.

- *We are being whipped into a new panic by an unholy alliance between ISIS and Fox News.* Both are presenting events currently underway in Syria, Iraq and now Libya as moments in a Holy War, and as a replay of the Crusades. We need calmer counsel to prevail. Cleveland is not under attack. By endlessly criticizing the President for not labeling ISIS as "Islamic terrorists," the journalists at Fox News regularly slide over the extent to which ISIS's main barbarities are inflicted on other Muslims—Shias—and discount the regularly demonstrated condemnation of ISIS by leading Islamic institutions and figures. And when O'Reilly, Hannity and their kind quote Graeme Wood's Atlantic article with such enthusiasm, they do more than stoke the flames of a growing Islamophobia here in America. They also reinforce what is the greatest weakness in the Wood piece: the impression created there that the ISIS reading of the Qur'an is the only possible accurate one, and that Islam as a whole is "literalistic, backward-minded, and arcane" when in truth it is none of those things. The President is right. Terrible things have been done in the past in the name of all religions, including Christianity; and terrible things are being done now by ISIS to other Muslims, and not just to Christians, in the areas which ISIS controls. So there is literally nothing to be gained by blaming every adherent to a particular religion for the excesses of a terrorist few. The alliance between Bill O'Reilly and the ISIS leadership is indeed an unholy one. The war they mutually advocate is equally unholy; and we need to say so.

The Electoral Politics Surrounding the Military Campaign

It is because the arguments for scaling back US military involvement in the fight against ISIS are so much more convincing than those for persisting in our present course—let alone more convincing than those for increasing our military involvement—that current political developments in and around Washington DC should concern us greatly.

The counter-arguments to war need to be aired—in as strong and regular a manner as possible—precisely because of the electoral and governmental consequences of staying silent. For we are into the next presidential election cycle, whether we like it or not; and the dynamic now emerging there is one that will—if not reversed—take the United states inexorably into yet more military adventurism in the Middle East. Why? Because each Republican presidential hopeful is currently outbidding the others in their hawkishness, with Lindsay Graham setting the pace; and we can expect Hillary Clinton—vulnerable as she is on Benghazi—to inevitably follow. And you only have to look at the list of foreign policy advisers surrounding the Republican front-runner—Jeb Bush—to see that the neo-cons are on the way back, and to realize that we face the possibility of history once as tragedy and twice as farce. Are we really happy to see Paul Wolfowitz and John Bolton back in positions of influence in Washington DC, after the mess they left behind the last time they were there? I sincerely hope that we are not.

Between now and the general election in 2016, we can expect leading Republican politicians to treat any manifestation of Presidential restraint by Barack Obama as further evidence of why ISIS is growing, rather than as a rational response to a complex problem that cannot be solved by American military means alone, let alone as a rational response to a complex problem that military means deployed too extensively can only make worse. We can also expect leading Democratic politicians to tack to that Republican wind, even though to do so will be both immediately electorally damaging and, over the longer period, internationally dangerous. We saw what happened to Democratic candidates when the whole party tried to distance itself on the President ahead of the mid-terms. We don't need that distancing again.

What we need instead is a growing and sustained voice—within and beyond the Democratic Party—pressing for a resetting of the structure and practice of the anti-ISIS coalition: shifting its leadership into the hands of Arab governments; putting local military forces at the heart of the fight; redirecting American efforts into denying ISIS access to global social media; and establishing sharp (and ever increasing) limits on both the direct and indirect involvement of US military personnel in the fighting on the ground.

Solution: Build Peace, Don't Wage War

David Alpher

Working to make ISIS obsolete by improving the miserable lives of those they seek to recruit is the only sound plan to destroy the terrorist organization, according to the author of the following viewpoint. David Alpher, who serves as adjunct professor at George Mason University's School for Conflict Analysis and Resolution, asserts that military action only emboldens ISIS and weakens the environment for the people of the Middle East, thereby adding fuel to its fire. He claims that the ideal methods of resolution have been lost on those that make international policy decision in the United States.

Just this past weekend of July 4, US-led coalition aircraft targeted the ISIS stronghold of Raqqa in Syria. It was one of the "largest deliberate engagements to date," said a coalition spokesman, and it was executed "to deny [ISIS] the ability to move military capabilities throughout Syria and into Iraq." The scale of these responses gives a hint both to how concerned we are about such groups–and to how badly we misunderstand how to deal with them.

ISIS—the self-proclaimed "Islamic State"—is the monster of our times, our Grendel. Every pundit, commentator, armchair warrior and presidential candidate, declared and otherwise, claims to have a strategy to defeat them. A steady stream of political statements offering answers to "what do we do about them?" have gotten progressively more hawkish.

"Why defeating ISIS with military might is starry eyed idealism," by David Alpher, The Conversation, June 6, 2015. https://theconversation.com/why-defeating-isis-with-military-might-is-starry-eyed-idealism-43563. Licensed under CC BY-ND 4.0.

Would-be presidents have given us options ranging from bombing ISIS "back to the 7th Century" (Rick Santorum), increasing the number of American troops in the fight (Lindsey Graham), and "look for them, find them and kill them" (Marco Rubio, quoting an action movie).

Bold words…and every one of them will fail, because they are far too idealistic to work in reality. If the candidates want realism, they'll have to advocate something else: peacebuilding.

"War as utopian idealism" and "peacebuilding as hard-nosed realism" sounds like an absurd joke.

Here's why it isn't.

War is Just Politics By Other Means

Carl Von Clausewitz, one of history's foremost military strategists and right at the foundation of American strategic teaching, famously called warfare an "extension of politics by other means."

What he meant by that is that if military action is going to be successful, it cannot stand alone or direct itself. Unless it grows out of and complements a solid, sustainable political strategy, it will fail.

That was true in his day of formalized warfare; in today's world, it's even more critical an insight, because what the world faces in ISIS isn't a war among uniformed armies and sovereign nations.

This conflict and others like it around the world are rooted in people, not states. It's rooted in ideology and religion, in sectarian frictions, in political exclusion and social marginalization, in resources and access.

That's a long list of root causes and conditions that do not respond to force and cannot be bombed out of existence.

In other words, if "defeat ISIS" isn't couched within a clear, realistic plan to do the human, political, diplomatic and development work necessary to fix the problems that gave it rise, the mission will fail.

In its failure, it will leave behind the seeds of a new threat in fertile soil, just as ISIS itself grew from the roots of al-Qaeda even after the bloom was cut off above.

Peacebuilding, at its heart, means doing the hard work of correctly analyzing the causes and conditions that lead to violence and instability. It means identifying ways of breaking those causes down, and then doing the even harder work of helping to build healthy, resilient social and political structures in their place.

It's work that's usually dismissed as an exercise in starry-eyed, utopian idealism by a policy community dominated by the philosophy of nation states and Realpolitik. And yet over the last few years, the fallacy of that dismissal has become increasingly clear.

General James Mattis told Congress flatly that "if you don't fully fund the State Department, then I need to buy more ammunition." General Phipps, former commander of the 101st Airborne Division in Afghanistan, when asked about peacebuilding outreach to men he'd fought not long before, replied "That's how wars end... we can't kill our way out of this."

The Least Effective Tool Against Terrorism is War

Serious research centers have arrived at the same conclusion: the RAND Corporation, as far back as 2008, advised that outside military intervention is bar none the least effective way to make terrorist groups go away.

Ending the kind of conflicts we see most often today requires building inclusive governance and rule of law far more than it requires the defeat of a fighting force on the battlefield.

"Peacebuilding" is a broad category of work, which seeks to address the root causes of conflict and instability within populations and systems of governance. In conflicts that involve people more than states, any answer other than this shows a lack of understanding. Beginning now rather than waiting for the battlefield victory is an imperative, because it's only through *this* work that the next battle gets less likely.

In fact the battlefield options - however satisfying they may seem in a tactical sense - often cause more trouble than they're worth. The Saudis are discovering this in their campaign against the Houthis in Yemen, which is entirely military and has no parallel political component, and is having predictably destabilizing consequences.

Yes, building peace is a long process that will take years, perhaps generations; but those years will pass whether or not we recognize the need for a more realistic foreign policy, and the only question is whether in years to come progress has been made, or the war goes on.

The discussion about ISIS, as with many others around the globe, has lost track of realism. Instead of looking at the military as an extension of politics, speakers across the board have begun to look at politics as secondary - something to worry about once the hard work of fighting's done.

Practical Actions For Peace-Building

What does this look like in practice? Here are four possible actions:

One:
The "real battle" here isn't with ISIS, it's for the populations they're trying to sway. There is no understating the power of the following scenario: An American politician saying, in a public forum, "I speak now to all of the population caught up in this fight, be you Sunni, Shiite, Yazidi, Kurd or otherwise, and I say, 'It's not just *their destruction* we have in mind— it's *your survival.*"

ISIS may prove impossible to talk with, but if we're indiscriminate and also ignore the population who is looking to the outside world for engagement and help, we're doing nothing but feeding into the vicious cycle.

Two:
Make it clear to the populations concerned that we strive to address the problems *they* face, not just those symptoms of the problems that *we* face.

Speaking to the current fight but not the problems that gave rise to it and which will still exist once the smoke clears just comes across as naive and disingenuous. Make a clear statement, for example, that we will not support repressive regimes in exchange for expedient stability, but are prepared for the long haul of achieving stability through unfailing support for the ideals of inclusive good governance that we ourselves hold dear.

Three:

My research and personal experience working for organizations in the region as well as many years spent in conflict-affected areas have shown me repeatedly that the real key to peace-building (as with development overall) isn't "what you do," it's "how you do it."

The most effective "how" is to look past states to see people, and provide incentives to get the population and government alike involved in designing and negotiating their own inclusive way forward - with our *support*, but not with our *direction*. Helping to build connectivity between the two—defined through trust, partnership and locally negotiated outcomes—is a powerful programmatic outcome.

It's also a good working definition of "good governance," and a more terrifying thought for ISIS than any weaponry can be.

Four:

Most of all, recognize that the military neither can nor should be the primary vehicle for American engagement overseas, and reprioritize funding accordingly.

The military is not trained for the jobs that peace-building entails, but USAID, the State Department and most importantly non-governmental organizations, are.

The message we send by prioritizing our own national security agenda while underfunding the agencies whose core mission and skillset is to work with good governance, justice, peace and livelihoods, is that we have no intention of doing more than eradicating symptoms while leaving the causes unchecked.

The military does have its role to play in winning a battle, but if "war" is our only lens, we will see only battlefield solutions to a set of problems that can't be solved with those. If we want to end the problem, we need to speak to the broad population with those tools that bring life, not death.

At some point an American president will be forced to recognize that fixing problems like the ones in Iraq and Syria is too complicated to sum up in a campaign slogan or sound bite. That's the hard truth.

The only question is how much in blood, time and treasure will be wasted before this realization hits home.

Getting rid of ISIS and groups like it certainly requires seriousness and a willingness to get hard work done—but that doesn't just mean preparing to get bloody. It means we need to be realistic and unafraid to say, "Our strategy is to build peace."

Best Bet to Beat Syria: Take It to Court!

Matthew Fitzpatrick

The following viewpoint comes from Flinders University associate professor of international history Matthew Fitzpatrick, who asserts that the base desire for a military solution to the conflict in Syria must be overcome by a more practical and peaceful resolution based on the efforts of the International Criminal Court. The Court, claims Fitzpatrick, can bring to trial and convict Syrian leader Basher al-Assad of crimes against humanity if he indeed has been found guilty of using poison gas on his own people.

The gassing of civilians by a military force is a crime and those who order it and carry it out are criminals who should be brought to trial.

The international community has such a court—the International Criminal Court—an institution which now has the world's more brutal political and military leaders looking over their shoulder for fear they might be extradited to the Hague to answer for their crimes.

If Bashar al-Assad is found to have used poisonous gas on his own population, as almost certainly seems to have been the case, then he must be put on trial for crimes against humanity.

This, however, is a world away from the notion that the international community should militarily intervene in the uncontrolled violence of the Syrian civil war.

"Five Reasons Military Intervention in Syria Is Wrong," by Matthew Fitzpatrick, ABC News, August 28, 2013. Reprinted by Permission.

The situation is complex, but at its simplest, here are five reasons why military intervention in Syria would be the wrong response to the most recent gas attacks.

1. As the recent wars in Afghanistan and Iraq have demonstrated, the civilian death toll from external military intervention quickly comes to exceed that which prompts the intervention in the first place. Killing more Syrians than the Assad regime itself is no way to pay tribute to those killed by their own government.

2. Within Syria there is no military power that would welcome or support external military intervention, particularly from Europe or the United States. While the beginnings of the 'Arab Spring' phase of the civil war saw some Syrians engaged in a struggle for a democratic Syria, these voices have been drowned out by the sound of the weapons fired from rival militias. Alongside Assad's troops, Hezbollah and Iranian military troops are fighting Lebanese Salafists, Al Qaeda and the ultra-Islamist al-Nusra Front. The only thing that all of these groups have in common is that they would welcome the opportunity to attack Western armies, no matter how altruistic their underlying motivations might be.

3. Internationally, there is no consensus that would offer a risk-free intervention. With Russia's Vladimir Putin still deeply supportive of Assad (although Saudi Arabia is attempting to lure him away with the promise of oil) and China strongly opposed to external intervention, there is virtually no chance of a UN mandate sanctioning military action. Unilateral action by Britain, France or the United States against Syria would risk broadening the conflict into another Cold War, while also inviting regional players such as Iran, Israel, Saudi Arabia, Turkey or even Russia to become even more heavily involved than they currently are. Such a broadening of the conflict is in nobody's interests.

Raising the Stakes in Syria

[...]

Why would Iranian forces in direct combat in Syria matter? First, it would represent an historic development and perhaps a change in military doctrine. For the first time since the Iran-Iraq War of the 1980s, IRGC units could be acting as an expeditionary force rather than the usual advise, train, equip and proxy-build mission. Even if this shift is out of necessity, the rest of the Middle East now must worry about battle hardened Iranian forces willing to fight in the open across borders, rather than only by proxy in the shadows.

Second, it indicates the depth of Tehran's and Damascus' problems in mounting a sufficient force to secure defendable Syrian territory. It is reasonable to assume that Iran would rather not expend its elite IRGC fighters, but there may no longer be a choice. This relatively small IRGC deployment could be the test case for a larger escalation if needed.

Third, it may reflect the operational and strategic demands of Russia's intervention. Operationally, Putin may have insisted on the new Iranian forces to help ensure a victory on the ground before committing his air force. Strategically, Russia is also likely to have different end states than Iran in mind. Russia may be more willing to sacrifice Assad, Damascus, or the emerging Iranian position against Israel in the Golan Heights, if it ensures a settlement that retains Putin's interests and naval base along the Mediterranean Coast. Tehran's escalation may be a response to concerns of losing strategic control to Russia, and an effort to ensure Iranian leverage in any negotiations.

What is likely even more concerning to Quds Force Commander Qassem Soleimani and Iranian Supreme Leader Ayatollah Ali Khamenei is whether this new deployment will be enough to satisfy Putin's expectations and turn the tide for Assad. The IRGC is already in unchartered territory. If the fight in Aleppo and elsewhere stalls for more than a couple of months, who knows what steps Iran take next?

- "This Is How Iran Just Raised the Stakes in Syria," by J. Matthew McInnis,
  The National Interest, October 23, 2015.

4. Intervention would only make sense in the context of an attempt to achieve concrete political or military objectives. None beyond 'something must be done' or 'there is a need to respond to a provocation' has been offered. There is no plan for stopping the multidirectional violence, much less rebuilding the nation. Simply bombing Damascus or Aleppo to assuage the conscience of the West that they 'did something' seems like the worst form of symbolic politics.

5. Perhaps more abstractly, a civil war is the most fundamental and brutal attempt to answer the question of who exercises the monopoly on the control of violence that underwrites the power of the state. Artificially inflating the power of one favoured but weaker faction to seize control of the state invites later challenges to this power in the not too distant future. Unless an indefinite guarantee of military support for the weaker faction is offered, that weaker faction (no matter how enlightened) cannot realistically be expected to maintain control over the state. The utter lawlessness in many regions of Libya today is the most recent example of what happens when outside powers back weak forces they deem to be on the right side of history in a civil war.

There is something superficially appealing about the notion of the legions of freedom on the march, overthrowing the forces of oppression. Events are rarely that simple.

In the case of Syria, it is certainly not the case that military action will offer a straightforward righting of wrongs. Rather, military action invites a series of unintended knock-on effects which could escalate the Syrian conflict in such a way as to endanger the lives of far more Syrian civilians.

All About the Syrian Refugee Crisis

Max Fisher and Amanda Taub

The horrific humanitarian crisis in Syria, which has caused a flood of refugees to pour into other European countries, has raised thousands of questions. The two writers of the following viewpoint seek to provide knowledge to their readers for a better understanding of the catastrophic events that led to the flight from Syria and other Middle Eastern nations, the plight of the refugees, and the both warm and cold receptions they have received in the nations of Europe (and elsewhere) in which they have landed.

There have always been refugees: people who are forced from their home countries by conflict or repression or something else, and who must find new homes and new lives abroad. But there is something different about what's happening now. The world is experiencing a crisis more severe than anything it has seen in decades—and we are just beginning to wake up to what that means.

Make no mistake: The current refugee crisis is global. The coverage has focused heavily on the refugees arriving in Europe, and especially on Syrian refugees. But in fact refugees are fleeing countries from Honduras to Nigeria to Myanmar, and they are arriving in wealthy countries including the US and Australia, as well as poorer ones like Turkey and Lebanon. It is a worldwide problem—one whose scale and severity is unmatched since World War II.

"The Refugee Crisis: 9 Questions You Were Too Embarrassed to Ask," by Max Fisher and Amanda Taub, Vox Media, September 9, 2015. Reprinted by Permission.

What follows is a straightforward explanation of the very basics of the refugee crisis: the key facts you need to know to understand what's happening, how the crisis became so severe, and what can be done to fix it.

1) What is the refugee crisis?

At its most basic level, the refugee crisis is driven by a single fact: There are 19 million people in the world who are currently refugees—a disastrously high number—and they all need to find somewhere they can live in safety.

But when we talk about the global refugee crisis, we're not just talking about numbers. We're really talking about the ways in which nations fail refugees. That happens at four distinct stages—all of them terrible in their own way. All refugees go through at least one of those terrible steps, but the most vulnerable people, if they do ever manage to reach safety at all, are likely to go through all four.

Refugees and migrants arriving by sea in Europe (2014 and 2015)

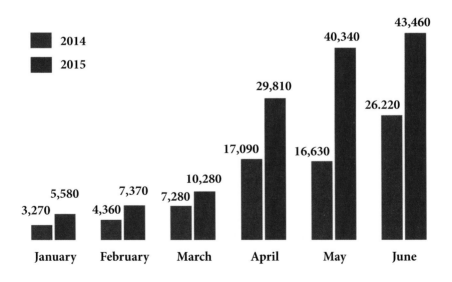

Source: Governments, UNHCR/29 June 2015

The first step of the refugee crisis is the persecution that forces refugees to flee their homes in the first place. Some are fleeing war, some political persecution, and some other kinds of violence, but all refugees, by definition, experience this. Today Syria's civil war is especially dire. But it's not the only cause of the global refugee crisis, which is being driven by a host of national crises taking place around the globe, many of which are totally unconnected to one another. There are wars in Somalia and Afghanistan and Libya, lower-level violence in Central America and Nigeria and Pakistan, persecution in Eritrea and Myanmar and Bangladesh, and so on.

The second step is what happens to those refugees once they are forced out of their homes: Often, though not always, they end up in camps. Life in the camps is often difficult, cramped, and unsafe, with few prospects for work or education. This is a crisis for the refugees as well for as the countries that house them; for instance, host countries like Lebanon and Turkey are struggling to manage their camps for refugees and to absorb the thousands or even millions of people who live in them. These camps are a global failure: The UN is far short of the $8.4 billion it says it needs to provide bare minimum services just for Syrian refugees. And they are also national failures: They keep refugees from integrating into the local communities and creating stable, productive new lives there. At their worst, camps can keep families stuck in limbo for generations.

The third step is what happens when refugee families, perhaps after seeing that the camps offer them little hope or protection, seek out safety from persecution further afield, often in developed countries, particularly in Europe. The journey is often horrifyingly dangerous: Many families drown crossing the Mediterranean in rickety boats, for example, which is why a Syrian toddler's body washed up on a Turkish beach last week. The families understand the risk, and may pay thousands of dollars per person for the trip, but often feel it is their only option. The trip is so perilous in part because Western governments, wanting to discourage all forms of uncontrolled migration, have let it be that way as a matter of deliberate policy.

The fourth step is the one that many Western countries are experiencing now: what happens when large numbers of refugees show up. Often, they face systems that are badly broken—the squalid overcrowded camps in Greece, for example—or that are overtly hostile to refugees in an effort to keep them out. This is changing a little bit, but most European countries are still trying to keep refugees out and refusing to accept even a remotely sufficient number of them for resettlement, which means the families who make it to Europe end up in camps, sleeping in train stations, or living in fear of deportation.

This last step of the crisis is about much more than just funding: It's forcing some really sensitive political issues to the surface in Europe, over migration and identity and the future of the European Union. Until Europeans can figure out those issues, hundreds of thousands of refugees will continue to suffer.

2) Why are there so many refugees right now?

There's no single reason, because a number of the crises driving people from their homes are not connected. There's no real link, for example, between the war in Afghanistan and the persecution of the Rohingya minority in Myanmar, or between violence in Nigeria and violence in Honduras and El Salvador.

But there is one thing that jump-started the crisis, and that has helped to make it so especially bad: the Arab Spring. It began in 2011 as a series of peaceful, pro-democracy movements across the Middle East, but it led to terrible wars in Libya and Syria. Those wars are now helping to fuel the refugee crisis.

It's not hard to understand why Syrians are fleeing. Bashar al-Assad's regime has targeted civilians ruthlessly, including with chemical weapons and barrel bombs; ISIS has subjected Syrians to murder, torture, crucifixion, sexual slavery, and other appalling atrocities; and other groups such as Jabhat al-Nusra have tortured and killed civilians as well. The civil war has killed a shocking

250,000 people, displaced half of the population, and caused one in five Syrians (4 million people) to flee the country.

Libya's role in the refugee crisis is different: The war there is terrible, but it has not displaced nearly as many people. What it has done, however, is open up a long-closed route from Africa to Europe.

For years, the EU kept refugees out of sight and out of mind by paying Libyan dictator Moammar Gadhafi's government to intercept and turn back migrants that were heading for Europe. Gadhafi was something like Europe's bouncer, helping to bar refugees and other migrants from across Africa. His methods were terrible: Libya imprisoned migrants in camps where rape and torture were widespread. But Europe was happy to have someone else worrying about the problem.

When Libya's uprising and Western airstrikes ousted Gadhafi in 2011, Libya collapsed into chaos. The route through Libya—and, from there, across the Mediterranean—suddenly opened, though it remained dangerous. As a result, the number of people making the perilous journey to Europe climbed considerably.

There is another reason that this crisis is so severe: Politics within Europe are unusually hostile to refugees and migrants at the moment. That isn't causing the numbers of refugees to actually increase, of course, but it's part of why the refugees are in crisis, stuck in camps or dying in the Mediterranean rather than resettling safely in Europe. There are a few reasons anti-refugee and anti-migrant politics are rising in Europe (more on this below), but it's making it harder for Europe to deal with the crisis, and many refugee families are suffering as a result.

3) Why is there a war in Syria, and why is it so terrible?

Here, from Zack Beauchamp, is the briefest, simplest way we can describe this complex, horrific war:

Syria is a relatively new country: Its borders were constructed by European powers in the 1920s, mashing together several ethnic and religious groups. Since late 1970, a family from one of those smaller groups—the Assads, who are Shia Alawites—has ruled the country in a brutal dictatorship. Bashar al-Assad has been in power since 2000.

This regime appeared stable, but when Arab Spring protests began in 2011, it turned out not to be. Syrians were clearly sick of the country's corruption, brutality, and inequity. Protests began that spring. Though the protests weren't about sectarian issues, many of the protesters were from the country's largest demographic group, the long-disadvantaged Sunni Arabs.

On March 18, Syrian regime forces opened fire on peaceful protestors in the southern city of Deraa, killing three. Protests grew, as did the increasingly violent crackdowns. Assad's troops shot demonstrators en masse, abducted and tortured activists, and even murdered children.

Perhaps inevitably, Syrians took up arms to defend themselves. Defectors from Assad's regime joined them. By early 2012, the protests had become a civil war. Government forces indiscriminately bombed and shelled civilian populations; Assad aimed to crush the rebels and their supporters by brute force.

Assad deliberately targeted Syria's Sunni Muslim majority, civilian and rebel alike. His goal was to polarize the conflict on religious lines, to turn what began as a broad-based uprising against a dictator into a sectarian war, with religious minorities on his side. He knew this would attract extremists to the rebel side, which would make the world afraid of seeing Assad lose.

It worked. By 2013, hard-line Sunni Islamists had become some of the most effective anti-Assad fighters, backed by Sunni states like Saudi Arabia and Qatar. Iran's Shia government backed Assad with cash, weapons, and soldiers. The conflict became, in part, a Middle East sectarian proxy war of Shia versus Sunni.

Meanwhile, a Sunni extremist group known as al-Qaeda in Iraq, which had been mostly defeated in 2007, was rebuilding itself. It grew strong fighting against Assad in Syria, and later swept northern Iraq under the new name ISIS.

By 2014, Syria was divided between government, rebel, ISIS, and Kurdish forces. (The Kurds, an ethnic minority, have long sought independence.) It is divided in a terrible stalemate.

[...]

Civilians always suffer most in war, but Syria's have suffered especially. Assad targets them ruthlessly, including with barrel bombs and chemical weapons. ISIS and other groups, when they take over towns, put them under brutal and violent rule. Fighting has flattened entire neighborhoods and towns.

Most of Syria's 4 million refugees have ended up in overcrowded and underfunded camps in neighboring countries. But with little hope of returning home, many are seeking new lives in Europe, though the journey is expensive, uncertain, and often fatal. That they would risk so much speaks to the horrors they're fleeing, and to their hopes, however faint, of finding a future for their children.

4) Why is the journey so dangerous?

There are two culprits: the exploitative criminal networks that move the refugees for high fees but offer them little safety, and the Western governments that have tolerated these dangers, at times as part of a deliberate effort to discourage refugees from attempting the journey.

Last fall, for instance, the UK cut funding for the Mare Nostrum search-and-rescue operations that saved an estimated 150,000 people in one year, saying the rescues encouraged more people to make the crossing. The Italian government ended the operation in November. Since then, it has been replaced by the EU's far more limited Frontex program, which only patrols within 30 miles of the border and does not have a search-and-rescue mission.

The result, predictably, has been deadly: An estimated 2,500 people have already died so far this summer. This is not an accident. It is the result of European policy meant to keep out refugees. But, again, this isn't just a European phenomenon—the pattern looks pretty similar in other rich countries, as well.

Australia, for example, has gone to great lengths to prevent so-called "boat people" from reaching its shores, including imprisoning them in abusive detention centers on remote Pacific islands, and shipping them off to Cambodia.

In North America, the US has stepped up enforcement efforts after last year's child migrant crisis, including sending aid to Central American countries in exchange for efforts to keep children from making the journey to the United States. As with Europe and other countries, the whole idea is to keep refugees from showing up in the first place—even though these efforts never solve, and often don't even address, the underlying crises that cause the refugees to flee in the first place.

5) Why are Western countries making it so difficult for refugees to come?

Some of this is about issues that are particular to the US and to Europe and Australia, but there is also a generalized anti-immigration sentiment playing out across the developed countries where refugees are arriving.

Europe, like a lot of places, has pretty robust anti-immigration politics. The British tabloid press, for example, has for years scaremongered about the supposed threats from refugees and migrants. Such politics, in Europe or elsewhere, often get described as being about pure racism or xenophobia, but in fact they're about something a little different: a fear, rarely articulated, of changing demographics and civic identity.

Taking in large numbers of refugees requires accepting that those refugees might bring changes to your nation's identity or culture. And while that change is often economically and culturally enriching, it can still feel scary. It requires people to modify, ever so slightly, their vision of what their town and neighborhood look like. That change can be hard to accept. You can see this play out in Europe, for example, in the regular political backlashes against new mosques being constructed. Those backlashes are partly about

Islamophobia, but they are also an expression of people's fear and insecurity about "losing" what made their community feel familiar.

And anti-immigration sentiment tends to rise when people feel economically insecure, as many do in Western countries now. This insecurity can bring a sense of zero-sum competition, even though in fact migration is typically economically beneficial. There is thus enormous political demand within Western countries for keeping out migrants and refugees.

6) Why is Europe so unwelcoming to the refugees?

Refugees are showing up just as the European Union is in the middle of a pretty fraught debate over migration, which is part of the EU's growing political tension over the feasibility of the Union itself.

In the 1990s, the EU introduced something called that Schengen Area that allows near-unlimited migration between EU countries. It's worked well, but not everyone is comfortable with the influx, and the backlash has contributed to right-wing, anti-EU parties in Europe. This gets expressed as generalized hostility against migrants. If you're a politician in, say, France, then you can't call

Top 5 nationalities arriving by sea in Europe

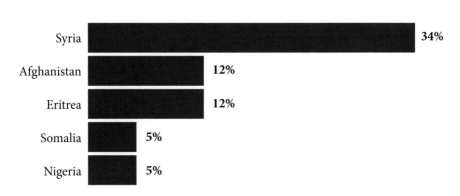

Source: Governments, UNHCR/29 June 2015

for kicking out the Poles—that would violate EU rules—but you can call for keeping out Nigerian refugees.

European countries are also taking advantage of EU rules to keep refugees out. In theory, the EU's open internal borders mean that it ought to handle refugees collectively. But in practice, most EU member states don't want to take their fair share, and EU rules mean they don't technically have to. Part of how this happens is a European Union rule called the Dublin Regulation, which requires refugees to stay in the first European country they arrive in until their asylum claims are processed. This rule has allowed Europe to push most of the burden onto Greece and Italy, which are overwhelmed with thousands of refugees.

At the same time, countries such as Hungary and Austria are tightening their borders with other European countries to keep refugees from crossing their territory, even en route to other countries like Germany. In Hungary's case, this is apparently intended to discourage refugees from entering the EU at all—Hungarian Prime Minister Victor Orban is openly hostile to refugees, who he believes are a threat to Europe's "Christian character." While Germany has dramatically relaxed its asylum rules, which is a very important step for dealing with the crisis and helping refugees, the rest of Europe has not really followed, and is tightening restrictions rather than loosening them.

Until the EU can take on the refugee crisis collectively, as it's supposed to, the problem will remain unsolved. But the EU may be incapable of coming together on this until it is able to deal with its underlying issues over the Union and whether individual states are really willing to give up a little bit of their separateness to function better together.

7) Why isn't America taking more Syrian refugees?
The US is usually pretty good about resettling refugees—it resettles about 70,000 a year—but has so far badly lagged in resettling Syrians. Since 2011, the UN refugee agency has referred

17,000 Syrians to the US for resettlement, but the US has only resettled about 9 percent of those.

The US process for applying for resettlement can take up to 24 months for Syrians, due in part to extensive background checks and enormous paperwork requirements. The US can get away with imposing a long, painstaking bureaucratic process because it is voluntarily resettling Syrian refugees who are an ocean away. By contrast, countries that are confronting large groups of refugees who arrive in their territory and request asylum, as Europe is now, do not have that luxury. They cannot legally deport refugees with valid asylum claims, and so in most cases they have to let them stay until their cases have been decided.

But America's bureaucratic resettlement process, like its low acceptance rate for Syrian refugees, comes down in many ways to a fear of terrorism.

"The Obama administration has provided virtually no assurances that the admission of Syrian refugees will not pose a national security threat to the United States," Rep. Michael McCaul, who chairs the Homeland Security Committee, told the New Republic. "If anything, in speaking with leaders in executive branch departments and agencies, I have grown more concerned that we do not have the ability to confidently vet the Syrian refugee population for potential threat actors."

The joke is that the US won't give your family asylum if you once sold falafel to a jihadist, but the darkly humorous punchline is that it's not really a joke at all: The tolerance for "affiliation" with extremists is basically zero, even though it's just about impossible to survive in Syria today without interacting with extremists in some way.

McCaul and some other Republicans have warned that ISIS could exploit any Syrian refugee resettlement program to use as "a federally funded jihadi pipeline."

The Obama administration knows this isn't true—these are families stuck in camps we're talking about—but it is unwilling to overcome the political opposition. And as with the White House's failure to close Guantanamo, a big factor here is probably a fear of being blamed for a terrorist attack if one were to eventually occur. If the US were to admit, say, 65,000 Syrian refugees, as some humanitarian organizations have called for it to do, and just one of them were to be involved in some sort of attack, then it seems likely the Obama administration would face a severe political backlash.

So while many Americans today say they want the US to resettle Syrian refugees, they have also sent a very clear message that they fear terrorism above almost all else. US leaders have good reason to believe that if even one resettled Syrian committed extremism-tinged violence, they would pay a heavy political cost. The Obama administration appears, at the moment, more concerned with protecting itself against this perceived political risk that with saving the lives of thousands of Syrian families.

8) What's the difference between refugees and migrants?

Not everyone who is crossing the Mediterranean or otherwise showing up at a European or American border is a refugee; many are migrants coming for other reasons. That gets to the distinction between refugees and migrants.

Refugees are people who have been forced out of their home country against their will. The word "migrant" can mean someone who moves to a foreign country voluntarily, or it can be used as a broader umbrella term that includes refugees as well as voluntary migrants. For example, a Syrian man fleeing war is a refugee, whereas a Cameroonian man seeking economic opportunity is a migrant.

Whether someone is considered a refugee or a migrant effects what sorts of legal rights they have: Refugees can apply for asylum and are protected by international and domestic law, for example, while economic migrants cannot. There is no such thing as an "illegal asylum-seeker"—refugees can seek asylum in another country without obtaining a visa or resettlement authorization first. Economic migrants, by contrast, are usually required to have a visa or other form of work authorization in order to immigrate legally.

There is also a meaningful symbolic distinction between the words, one that often becomes political. Calling a group of people "refugees" can be a way of describing them as legitimately deserving of shelter and care, whereas calling them "migrants" can be a way of accusing them of arriving for economic reasons, and perhaps even lying about their asylum claims. This is why anti-immigration politicians will sometimes insist that a group of refugees are actually migrants who have come to exploit Western entitlement programs. And it is why, in this article and many others on Vox, you will see us use the word refugee rather than migrant when we are referring to people fleeing persecution.

But this distinction, for all its legal salience, is actually quite blurry—and it can also imply, wrongly, that non-refugee migrants should be rejected, that only refugees deserve their rights. Jørgen Carling, a scholar at the Peace Research Institute Oslo, put this well:

The 'two kinds of people' argument is further undermined by the drawn-out trajectories of many current migrants. A Nigerian arriving in Italy might have left Nigeria for reasons other than a fear of persecution, but ended up fleeing extreme danger in Libya. Conversely, a Syrian might have crossed into Jordan and found safety from the war, but been prompted by the bleak prospects of indeterminate camp life to make the onward journey to Europe. Regardless of the legal status that each one obtains in Europe, they are both migrants who have made difficult decisions, who deserve our compassion, and whose rights need to be ensured.

Drew Hinshaw, a West Africa–based reporter for the Wall Street Journal, elaborated on Twitter. "In many places I cover, asymmetrical war makes it hard to tell where war/poverty end/ begin," he wrote, citing as an example parts of Nigeria where low-level violence and bleak economic opportunities, combined, lead families to decide to try for a better life in Europe.

In such cases, of which there are a great many, the distinction between migrants and refugees—and the implied value of judgment of who does and does not "deserve" to seek a better life abroad— falls apart.

9) I want to help. What can I do?

There are a number of ways refugees are suffering, and thus a number of ways to help alleviate those specific traumas and injustices.

The United Nations refugee agency, UNHCR, is a few billion dollars short on funding just to administer aid to the millions of displaced Syrians. There are a number of excellent charities operating in conflict zones such as Syria and Afghanistan, as well as good governance organizations working to improve political conditions in countries where persecution and corruption contribute to refugee outflows.

There are also charities that help care for resettled refugees, or that provide them with legal council to seek asylum once they arrive in Europe or the US or elsewhere. These are all worthwhile causes that can help translate your time and money into ameliorating refugees' plight.

Ultimately, though, checkbook humanitarianism is not going to solve things. This crisis is about 19 million people who have been forced from their countries and need a new country to call home. Solving it will require resettling them, which will require the countries that can afford to absorb them to overcome their own political anxieties about large-scale immigration.

For those of us who live in those countries, that means accepting that our communities will look and feel different from how they have in the past. It requires adjusting, at least slightly, our vision of what our communities look like, and widening the definition of our culture to accommodate new arrivals, even if their customs and values might seem alien to us. That's not something that has ever come easily to people, but it is the only real solution there is.

Message to a Wannabe President: Aleppo Explained

Zack Beauchamp

When Libertarian presidential candidate Gary Johnson demonstrated what many perceived to be a shocking lack of knowledge of the Syrian refugee crisis in the fall of 2016, journalist Zack Beauchamp was motivated to explain to Johnson and others all about the humanitarian disaster. In the following viewpoint, Beauchamp writes about the devastating siege of the country, which forced Syrians to leave their home country to seek food, shelter, and safety. Beauchamp has established himself writing about politics for websites such as Vox, ThinkProgress, and the Dish.

During a Thursday appearance on MSNBC's *Morning Joe*, Libertarian presidential candidate Gary Johnson was asked about the city of Aleppo, the site of a major front in the Syrian civil war.

Johnson responded with a question: "What is Aleppo?"

This wasn't some kind of weird dodge—it's clear he actually doesn't know what Aleppo is. In a follow-up interview, Johnson was given a chance to explain himself. It didn't go well:

> *When you recognize what's going on in Syria, when you recognize that Aleppo is in kinda the epicenter between ... Aleppo! Umm, knowing that there's a city between the two forces, really at the epicenter, but not remembering or recognizing that that's Aleppo ... guilty.*

"Aleppo, Explained For Non-Experts and Gary Johnson," by Zack Beauchamp, Vox Media, September 8, 2016. Reprinted by Permission.

This is deeply embarrassing for the former New Mexico governor, who's been trying to position himself as the thinking conservative's alternative to Donald Trump.

But not everyone is running for president like Johnson is, so not everyone is expected to have snap answers handy about the complex Syrian civil war like Johnson should. Which means a lot of you out there probably have the same legitimate question: What is Aleppo, anyway, and why are people asking Johnson about it?

So here's a brief guide—to both the city's role in the Syrian conflict and why it's so important.

Aleppo is a city located in northwest Syria near the Turkish border. It's the capital of the eponymous Aleppo province, and was the country's most populated city before the war. Today it's perhaps the most significant battlefield in the defining conflict in Syria: fighting between Bashar al-Assad and various different anti-government rebel factions. (ISIS is not a major player in Aleppo City, though it has a presence in Aleppo province.)

Since Syria's 2011 Arab Spring protests descended into a civil war, Aleppo has been a major base for a number of different rebel factions opposed to the Assad regime. In September 2015, Assad's forces began a concerted effort to retake the city. The above map shows the government's progress: By December, they had made significant advances around the city and, by February 5, had nearly surrounded it.

Prior to the Aleppo offensive, Assad had been losing. In response, his international patrons—Russia and Iran—began increasing their support last fall. Their deployments allowed Assad's forces to make their major push toward the city.

"The operations in Aleppo Province have hinged upon heavy military support from both Russian warplanes and Iranian proxy fighters," Christopher Kozak, a research analyst at the Institute for the Study of War, wrote at the time. He continued:

Russia concentrated a significant portion of its air campaign against opposition forward positions and supply lines in Aleppo Province. Meanwhile, U.S. officials estimated in October 2015 that up to 2,000 Hezbollah, Afghan, and Iraqi Shi'a militia fighters led by Islamic Revolutionary Guard Corps (IRGC) – Quds Force commander Maj. Gen. Qassem Suleimani currently operated in Aleppo Province.

The worst-case scenario, at the time, was an all-out siege of the city's rebel-controlled eastern region, blocking even humanitarian assistance. This sort of siege is illegal under international law, but Assad has been doing it for years. That's because it works: Rebels who don't have food quickly lose the will to fight, and civilians in besieged areas will start cooperating with the government just to make it stop.

In July, these fears were realized. The Assad regime, with significant support from Iran, imposed a blockade on rebel areas, cutting off supplies to some 320,000 people.

At the end of July, the fractious rebel groups struck back, launching a rare coordinated offensive that caught the Assad regime off guard. By August 7, they had broken the siege of the city, allowing aid to flow in.

But the fighting didn't stop. You may have seen one of the images from the subsequent fighting: a little boy, named Omran Daqneesh, covered in dust and blood. Omran had been caught in a Russian airstrike in the city and was pulled out from under a building by rescuers.

While the rebels aren't nearly as responsible for Aleppo's pain, they're hardly saints themselves.

"The rebels include both jihadists formerly allied with Al Qaeda and commanders aligned with the Free Syrian Army, which has been supported sporadically by the Obama Administration," the New Yorker's Steve Coll writes. "The rebels fire inaccurately into government areas with improvised mortars that they call 'hell cannons.' The rounds include gas cylinders packed with explosives and metal shrapnel, designed to terrorize and maim."

More recently, the Assad regime has begun making gains again. On September 4, parts of eastern Aleppo were "re-besieged" by Assad's forces, taking advantage of divisions among the rebel groups. According to Charles Lister, a Syria expert at the Middle East Institute, Russian special forces were "centrally involved" in directing the offensive.

The Assad regime has advanced further since then, retaking the Ramousah district that rebels had used to establish a supply corridor. Wednesday afternoon, hours before Johnson's comments, it reportedly unleashed a major chlorine gas attack on a civilian-populated area. At least 120 people suffered gas inhalation; a 13-year-old girl named Hajer Kyali died.

So Aleppo isn't just one site of tragedy among many in Syria. It's a humanitarian crisis and one of the most important battlefronts in the country—the kind of thing that someone who wants to be president of the United States should at least have passing familiarity with.

What does the battle for Aleppo tell us about Syria?

This back and forth in Aleppo, where the rebels and Assad seem to trade gains and momentum, illustrates the fundamental seesaw dynamic of the civil war. The city is important not just in humanitarian terms but also because a candidate's approach to Aleppo is a microcosm for his approach to the entire conflict.

Assad had lost ground nationwide for most of 2015 before the Russian and Iranian escalations helped him launch the Aleppo offensive. For most of the two years prior to that, he appeared to have had the upper hand on the rebels—who, in turn, had looked likely to win for much of 2011 and 2012.

These shifts in momentum reflect the fundamental weakness of all parties.

Assad has manpower problems, the rebels are deeply divided, the Kurds have no ability to control a mostly Arab country, and ISIS has managed to make enemies out of virtually every powerful actor in the Middle East. No side is strong enough to crush any other by dint of force, so gains end up being pretty temporary.

Moreover, both Assad and the non-ISIS rebels are backed by actors outside of the country, who tend to escalate when it looks like their proxies are losing ground. The role of Russian special forces in the recent besiegement of Aleppo, seemingly a response to the rebel breaking of the siege, is a perfect example.

This creates a deadly seesaw effect, whereby Assad and the rebels keep trading territory without anyone ever gaining a permanent upper hand. This also makes any kind of peace deal even harder to negotiate: At any given point, either the regime or the rebels feel like they're winning on the battlefield. Whoever has the upper hand has no incentive to come to terms.

These conditions, and other, make Syria a nearly impossible conflict to resolve even by the grim standard set by other civil wars. "This is a really, really tough case," Barbara Walter, a UC San Diego expert on civil wars, told the New York Times's Max Fisher.

Aleppo poses the basic dilemma created by the situation—how should the US handle a war that it can't end, short of a massive invasion?—in miniature.

Should the United States try to break the Aleppo siege using its own military, and thereby risk open conflict with nuclear-armed Russia? Should it provide deadly weapons to the opposition, knowing that those weapons might make their way to civilian-killing jihadists or simply prolong the conflict? Or should it stay out, and risk hundreds of thousands of people being gassed and starved?

These are the cold, hard realities of Syria policy—perhaps the most difficult foreign policy challenge that our next president will face.

The fact that Johnson doesn't seem to know the first thing about it is ... well, it would be a bit troubling if he had any chance of winning.

CHAPTER 3

Is There a Blueprint for Peace in the Middle East?

Preface

I dealism or realism? Boldness or practicality? A quick fix or a slow and steady pace? What is the most effective road toward a peaceful solution in the Middle East?

History has produced many skeptics and few believers. The sheer number of conflicts between religious zealots—and between nations in the region—seems to preclude any possibility of a speedy peace process or resolution based on idealism. But how does one use logic and practicality to fight the zealots and dictators?

This chapter will explore some alternatives, including what many perceive as a pie-in-the-sky goal of one world government. The world has shrunk enough in recent decades to legitimately consider the possibility—an enormous task with tremendously positive rewards, particularly in the Middle East, which is the hottest of the hot spots on the planet. Many dismiss the notion of a world government as unworkable, yet negotiating or gaining a peace through military means has proven equally unworkable. The problems that must be addressed and fixed permanently are so numerous and so deeply rooted that finding common ground seems impossible.

Can Israel finally recognize the Palestinian state? Can Palestine and Middle Eastern countries such as Iran accept the Jewish state as a permanent and powerful resident in the region? Can the religious factions that have brought violence and intolerance to Iran, Iraq, Syria and other nations come together in the common cause of peace? Can terrorism be destroyed without bloodshed? Must theocracy come to a crashing end for tranquility to reign? Can women in the Middle East gain social and political equality without drastic changes to the Islamic religious structure? How would that affect the region?

The Arab Spring of 2011 proved that millions of Middle Eastern people yearn to create an environment of political reform and social justice. They sought a higher level of self-determination. Though the events did bring about some change, they have proven thus far to be only a historical hiccup. The violence and destruction that has plagued the Middle East for centuries, particularly since the establishment of Israel, continues unabated. With brutal terrorist groups like ISIS now in the mix, the chaos has only grown in magnitude.

One can only speculate on what the future holds in the Middle East and offer possibilities for how best to bring about peace. This chapter will address both the challenges and the changes ahead.

US to Iran: Don't Even Think About Attacking Israel

Raphael Ahren

In the following viewpoint, journalist Raphael Ahren, who works as a diplomatic correspondent for the Times of Israel, *reports on the 2015 promise of a senior American defense official that the United States will defend the Jewish state if it is attacked by Iran. The official adds that maintaining Israeli military superiority over hostile neighbors will remain an American foreign policy priorit and explains that the nuclear deal brokered in part by the United States should help ensure that Iran will be unable to pose a high-level threat to a country it has in the past threatened to destroy.*

The United States will defend Israel in the case of an Iranian attack against it, a senior American defense official said Monday, asserting Israel's right to self-defense and the administration's commitment to the Jewish state's military superiority in the Middle East.

The administration respects Israel's right to self-defense and will continue to ensure the Jewish state's qualitative military edge, the official told Israeli reporters, arguing that the nuclear deal that the US and five world powers signed with the Islamic Republic last month will make an Israeli military attack less probable.

"We have an ally relationship. The word 'ally' means something to us. It means that if you are attacked, we will defend you. That

"US Pledges to Defend Israel If Iran Attacks," by Raphael Ahren, The Times of Israel, August 03, 2015. Reprinted by Permission. Originally appeared in The Times of Isreal. www.timesofisreal.com.

is what an ally relationship means… We use that term sparingly," the senior defense official said.

"We think that this deal decreases the need and likelihood of an attack. That's why we signed it. We understand that military action is always an option. It's an option for the United States," the official said. "It's an option for Israel. But the goal is to have an agreement that makes a military attack less needed. But Israel has the right to self-defense. We understand that."

Washington is "appalled" about the Iranian leadership continuing to call for Israel's destruction, the representative said, but argued that such utterances should not deter the six world powers from supporting the nuclear accord.

"That is not the way countries should act in today's world," the official said of Iranian Supreme Leader Ayatollah Khamenei's calls for Israel's annihilation. "That doesn't mean we shouldn't sign a deal that helps decrease the likelihood of them becoming a nuclear state. That's the very reason we signed it."

The senior defense official, who accompanied US Secretary Ashton Carter during his recent visit to Israel, said that there had been no discussion during the trip of an American compensation package to assuage Israel's fears over the Iran deal.

"We talked about extensive cooperation and additional areas of focus for that cooperation. There was literally no discussion of a deal," the official said. The US is ready to discuss upgrading its annual defense aid to Israel even after the US Congress affirms the nuclear deal, the official added. American commitment to maintain "Israel's qualitative military edge started long before this deal and will continue long after this deal."

Speaking to the Israel Diplomatic Correspondents Association, the senior defense official said officials in Jerusalem had expressed concern over additional American military assistance to the Gulf States, but added that only Israel would receive the F-35 fighter jet.

"There is no sale of the F-35 to anyone other than Israel even contemplated at this time in the Middle East. So reports of the F-35 to Egypt are erroneous and incorrect," the official continued.

The Iran deal is meant only to stop Iran's bid for a nuclear weapon and does not claim to curtail the regime's support for terrorist organizations such as Hezbollah and Hamas, the senior official said, adding, however, that Washington has taken and will continue to take steps to counter that. "We can't talk about it publicly, but we have taken action to make it clear that we will not accept this kind of behavior, that provisional support."

Regardless of the agreement, the US is not expecting Iran "to radically change its behavior," the official said. "We are trying to curb off a critically important security issue—the nuclear issue—and bring that issue out into the open, bring some visibility and some transparency. We don't believe that Iran is transformed, that leadership wants peace and harmony. That does not mean we believe that Iran is somehow transformed, that their leadership somehow wants to create peace and harmony."

The senior defense official rejected Defense Minister Moshe Ya'alon's claim, made a few weeks ago in a conversation with Israeli reporters, that while Israel sees Iran as part of the problem, the US sees it as part of the solution.

"I don't think we see Iran as part of the solution right now," the official asserted. "Sure, we hope that at some point in the future they'll change their behavior, from the senior levels down, but in the meantime we are negotiating on a critical security issue and that is what this deal is about. I don't think that we have any illusion that Iran is going to radically change its role in the international community."

A delegation of the Israel Diplomatic Correspondents Association is currently in Washington for a series of briefings with senior administration officials, US lawmakers and Jewish community officials to learn more about the discussion surrounding the Iran deal and other issues of importance to the bilateral relations. The week-long trip, the first of its kind, was funded by the Ruderman Family Foundation. The meetings were arranged independently by the IDCA.

Israel-Palestine Talks Won't Bring Peace

Ian Bremmer

The following piece from 2013 is critical of President Obama's plans to negotiate a settlement between Israel and the Palestinians. Though political scientist Ian Bremmer praises the efforts to get both sides to discuss their differences, he considers success to be unlikely and, even if achieved, insignificant in comparison to the myriad other problems facing the Middle East. Among the most pressing issues he cites are a civil war in Syria and a growing nuclear threat in Iran. Bremmer, who is president of Eurasia Group, a leading global political risk research and consulting firm, claims as false the notion that fixing the relationship between the Israelis and Palestinians will bring peace to the region.

O n Monday, the Obama administration announced that Secretary of State John Kerry had convinced Israel and the Palestinian Authority to sit down for negotiations for the first time in three years. Coming out of Monday and Tuesday's meetings, Kerry announced a goal of working out a comprehensive peace agreement within nine months.

Simply reviving talks at all is a highly impressive achievement; getting both sides to the table would have been impossible without Kerry's relentless effort. But if the Obama administration thinks this will change the dynamic in the Middle East, it is mistaken for two reasons. First, the initiative is unlikely to succeed, and

---

"Israeli-Palestinian Talks Won't Fix The Middle East's Problems," by Ian Bremmer, Reuters, July 31, 2013. Reprinted by Permission.

second, even if it did, it would have little impact on other more immediately pressing Middle East conflicts.

It's not that pushing for an Israel-Palestine solution isn't a valiant cause—it's that there is a full tray of conflicts in the Middle East that exist independently from the Israel-Palestine question: the growing rifts in Egypt or Iraq, the Syrian crisis that has claimed over 100,000 lives, or Iran's nuclear program. Even Israel and Palestine themselves prioritize many other regional concerns over making any significant progress with each other.

Don't get me wrong—the chances of success are not zero. But no matter how legacy-defining a lasting breakthrough would be for Obama and Kerry, the odds are incredibly long. The Israeli-Palestinian peace process has started and stopped countless times before. So what are the biggest structural impediments to a deal?

Obama's envoy, former Israeli ambassador Martin Indyk, will only be speaking with representatives of Palestinians' Fatah party. Since Hamas' electoral victory in 2006, the territories have been divided into two entities, with Gaza in Hamas' hands and the West Bank under Fatah control. Fatah lacks the legitimacy at home to negotiate and later implement any final agreement with Israel; the exclusion of the more fundamentalist Hamas from the diplomatic process gives Hamas every incentive to undermine any possible deal. If we begin to see substantial progress, expect Hamas to scuttle it with a violent show of force.

Benjamin Netanyahu, buoyed by a strong economy and relative peace, has little incentive to back down during negotiations. Israel has continued its settlement expansion and flouted its borders as defined in 1967 with relative impunity. For the last decade or so, left-wing parties have been increasingly marginalized and the public has grown more disenchanted with the peace process; these trends have led to a more uncompromising center-right government that's less interested in negotiating a settlement with the Palestinians. Recently, Israel has released prisoners and somewhat halted settlement construction in advance of the talks, but that may just be a short-term favor to Kerry that reaffirms the United States' leverage and importance. It doesn't suggest Netanyahu is ready to do an about face on years of policy.

The administration is well aware of the huge hurdles that an Israel-Palestine solution faces. So then why is John Kerry forging ahead regardless?

The key lies in the mistaken belief that the Israel-Palestinian conflict remains the linchpin of a dysfunctional Middle East. As the thinking goes, without fixing this issue, nothing else of deep substance can be solved. Today, this is patently untrue. Peace between the Israelis and Palestinians would not unwind the Iranian nuclear program, mend Syria's sectarian hellscape, or put Egypt back together again. It wouldn't keep Iraq from drifting perilously closer to civil war. The Middle East is now filled with relatively independent crises, and few of them have to do with Israel (even if Israel is subject to their effects).

A more cynical possibility? It's more politically palatable to fail on Israel-Palestine than on anything else. As opposed to Egypt, where the United States is torn between the security benefits and secularism of the military versus the democratically-elected status of the Muslim Brotherhood, Israel-Palestine is a clearer brokerage deal where, at the least, the United States' good intentions can't be questioned. If Obama's learned anything over the last two terms, it's that low expectations are a president's best friend—they provide room to surprise, or, if things go poorly, room to scapegoat. And there is a long and prestigious list of those who have failed on Israel-Palestine before this administration decided to attempt the feat.

In getting the Israelis and Palestinians to the table—something that was a complete non-starter at the beginning of the year—John Kerry has demonstrated his remarkable savvy as a diplomat. That's all the more reason it's a pity that the talks are unlikely to gain traction—and even if they did, a breakthrough deal still wouldn't douse the conflicts that would burn on throughout the region.

Middle East Battles Revolve Around Religion

Oren Kessler

Foundation for Defense of Democracies deputy director Oren Kessler emphasizes in the following viewpoint that religion, not politics, remains the motivational force throughout the Middle East. He insists that the overall influence of religion in the Islamic world wields more power than any other factor. Kessler adds that that level of influence is not fully appreciated or understood by those in other parts of the globe, and that any attempt to remove religion from politics in Middle Eastern countries will prove unpopular and ultimately unsuccessful.

A meme is gaining traction within American government and media, and it goes like this: The conflicts of the Middle East aren't about religion. Jihadist violence? Garden-variety criminality, the president says. Young people flocking to ISIS? "Thrill-seekers," posits the secretary of state, who are desperate for "jobs," per a State Department spokeswoman. Iran's belligerence? A reaction to ostracization, a former embassy hostage insists. Sunni-Shiite bloodletting? Jockeying for power, the pundits conclude.

It's not just a false narrative, but a dangerous one. It's true that the Middle East offers no easy policy options: witness Syria, where the choice of sovereign increasingly appears to be between the Islamic State and Islamic Republic (but neither of which, we're told, takes Islam all that seriously). Still, if we're to even try to address the region's maladies, we have to first correctly diagnose its disease.

"The Middle East's Conflicts Are About Religion," by Oren Kessler, The National Interest, February 13, 2016. Reprinted by Permission.

It's not that religion is the only force at play. It's not that the ranks of jihadist groups don't also include common criminals, or that leaders never use religion to their own cynical ends (Saddam Hussein's Faith Campaign is one salient example). It's that these phenomena are relatively minor compared to the vast influence religious belief still wields across much of the Middle East and the broader Islamic world.

It is, of course, near impossible to empirically demonstrate the motivations behind human actions, whether individual or collective. That doesn't mean, however, that our only recourse is to project our own motivations onto societies for which they don't fit. The debate over the religiosity of groups like ISIS, or of regimes like Saudi Arabia or Iran, is largely confined to the Western chattering classes. In the Islamic Middle East, the influence of faith is more often than not taken as a given.

Polls are instructive. In 2013, Pew—one of the world's leading pollsters—conducted a survey of thirty-eight thousand people in thirty-nine Muslim-majority countries. The results showed an overwhelming majority backed the implementation of Islamic law, particularly in countries that are some of the primary hubs of terror groups: 99 percent in Afghanistan, for example, and 91 percent in Iraq.

On matters of identity, results have been comparable. In Pew's 2011 survey, 94 percent of respondents in Pakistan said they identify first as Muslims rather than Pakistanis. In Jordan, a Western-oriented country and close U.S. ally, three times as many identified primarily as Muslims. Even in comparatively secular Turkey (and, incidentally, in the United States), twice as many people identified more as Muslims than citizens of their respective countries.

For most Middle Eastern Muslims, it is a personal and professional third rail to call for the removal of religion from public life, let alone to call into question God's existence. In Egypt, according to Pew, just 6 percent of respondents said the Quran need not be consulted in drafting laws, while more than eight in ten said those who leave the faith should be stoned to death (the Palestinian Authority, Afghanistan and Pakistan yielded similar results). In these countries at least, the community of secular-minded individuals, let alone atheists, is exceedingly small. Why then we do conclude that it is precisely those most loudly trumpeting their religious convictions who belong to it? I see two factors at play.

First, most post-religious Westerners have never felt the pull of faith. The prospect that a mentally sound person—let alone billions of them—would let spiritual conviction guide their most consequential actions doesn't quite add up. So too the notion of religion as one's primary identity marker. We deem one's nation to be an entirely legitimate identity marker; indeed, it's the default option, and in this country, failure to take sufficient pride in being American is grounds for suspicion. The prospect that faith, or even membership in a faith community, could fill that role rings hollow.

Second, from a policy perspective, nonreligious motives are more comforting. Addressing terrestrial motivations (money, land, grievance) is far easier than confronting a person's closest-held beliefs and the immutable scripture that underlies them. That's particularly the case because scrutinizing specific religious doctrines remains one of the last great taboos, all the more so when the faith in question is the supposedly non-white creed of Islam.

That's why even when religion is conceded to be at play, the assumption among right-thinking people is that faith is being "twisted" or "used" for some ulterior motive. Rarely considered is the possibility that billions of people take religion seriously and do their best to follow its precepts—precepts that can lead just as easily to charity and loving-kindness as to tribalism and terror.

On January 4, *Vox* published a lengthy article on the Saudi-Iranian rivalry that concluded, predictably, that "it's not really about religion." The very next day, the same author published a similar piece that offered this: "No one who seriously studies the Middle East considers Sunni-Shia sectarianism to be a primarily religious issue." That article approvingly cited a video by the Washington-based Al Jazeera anchor Mehdi Hasan, asserting that faith-based sectarian conflict is a "myth" and that regional rivalries are actually about "power, not piety."

It's particularly rich for Hasan to dismiss the very notion of sectarianism's sway. In an undated YouTube video (it's since been scrubbed from the Internet but a description is here), Hasan, who is Shiite, descends into a prolonged, tearful wail when recounting the story of the seventh-century Battle of Karbala, a formative moment in Shiite history in which Muhammad's grandson Hussain was killed. In another, he describes "*kuffar*" (non-Muslims) as "cattle. . . animals bending any rule to fulfill any desire" (that video is still online). So much for Hasan's pieties, as it were, over the power of faith and faction.

Nearly a year ago, Graeme Wood authored an *Atlantic* cover piece, "What ISIS Really Wants," propounding the apparently revolutionary notion that the group is driven by genuine religious fervor, and that its fire is based on a literal reading of Islamic texts.

The backlash was swift. In the same outlet, Wood was condemned for demonizing Muslims, and in the *New Yorker* for playing into the hands of extremists. Last month, responding to the second *Vox* piece, Wood tweeted: "Thought experiment: if these conflicts *were* about 'ancient religious hatreds,' how would they be different?"

It wasn't so long ago that Westerners took religion seriously. The Crusades, the Inquisition and Europe's wars of religion were about a lot of things—power, dynastic politics, land—but they were also genuinely, inseparably, *fundamentally* about religious belief. Barely a century ago, religion guided the lives of Westerners just as it does in much of the Islamic world today. For hundreds of millions in America it still does, and those Americans are rarely the ones asking whether the doctrinal devotion of most ISIS fighters, Saudi sheikhs or Iranian mullahs is a sham.

The rest of us are increasingly expected to nod to certain shibboleths: that power, money, resources and hegemony are the stuff of human motivation and, by extension, of international relations. Belief, after all, isn't—for the simple reason that it isn't for us.

VIEWPOINT 4

It's All About Islam

Jan Willem van der Hoeven

In the following viewpoint, International Christian Zionist Center director Jan Willem van der Hoeven expresses a cynical view of Islamists and their intentions to make peace with Israel and establish secular political agendas. He asserts that the problems in the region are rooted in Islam and that the fanaticism of its followers makes finding peaceful solutions to the myriad issues facing the Middle East impossible. The author, who has lived in the Middle East for more than 45 years, sees religious zealots as willing to kill in the name of Islam and Allah with little regard to the sanctity of human life.

B ecause of the humanistic and mainly secular mindset of the West, also of the major part of Israel's population, the following will be difficult to accept and digest, and that is: The chief reason for the Middle East conflict is not so much a secular political one, but a religious Islamic one!

Because the West nor Israel, generally speaking, does not want to be seen as being against another man's religious beliefs there is a widespread reluctance to face up to this problem. It is not done in our so-called tolerant society to criticize the tenants of a whole religion which comprises one billion adherents, and yet it is impossible to really solve the present Middle East conflict without facing up to this overall problem.

This is what this essay is purportedly trying to do. It will be in some ways difficult, but it is highly necessary. Because Islam

"The Main Reason for the Present Middle East Conflict: Islam and not 'The Territories,'" by Jan Willem van der Hoeven, Joseph Katz. Reprinted by Permission.

believes that it is the final revelation of Allah, superseding all previous ones, it has a high built-in characteristic of intolerance.

From the main religions it is indeed the youngest and thus the latest one and therefore it can easily claim without too much fear of contradiction that it is the final and more superior revelation of God. This being so, Islam has conveniently divided the whole world into two spheres: '*Dar al-Harb*' and '*Dar al-Islam*.' Dar al-Islam being the house or region of peace that means all lands and peoples already conquered by Islamic forces; and Dar el Harb being those lands and people in the world that still need to be conquered by Islam which is therefore the whole remaining world.

In *The Dhimmi* Bat Ye'or writes (page 45):

The jihad is a global conception that divides the peoples of the world into two irreconcilable camps: that of the dar al-Harb, the "Territory of War," which covers those regions controlled by the infidels; and the dar al-Islam, "the Territory of Islam," the Muslim homeland where Islamic law reigns. The jihad is the normal and permanent state of war between the Muslims and the dar al-Harb, a war that can only end with the final domination over unbelievers and the absolute supremacy of Islam throughout the world.

Once the forces of Islam conquer a land or territory, it is to remain under Islamic dominion forever ('for generations'), and it is a mortal affront to the supremacy of Islam when such territories would ever be lost to the dominion of Islam and revert to previous—infidel—ownership as was the case in Palestine. It was a Muslim controlled territory (under the Muslim Turks and later the Muslim Arabs) and reverted by the decree of the U.N. resolution back to its previous owners: the Jews.

This is how the Covenant of the Islamic Resistance Movement spells it out in several passages:

"Israel will exist and will continue to exist until Islam will obliterate it, just as it obliterated others before it." (The Martyr, Imam Hassan el-Banna)

"The Islamic Resistance Movement believes that the land of Palestine is an Islamic Waqf consecrated for future Muslim generations until Judgement Day. It, or any part of it, should not be squandered; it, or any part of it, should not be given up. Neither a single Arab country nor all Arab countries, neither any king or president, nor all the kings and presidents, neither any organization nor all of them, be they Palestinian or Arab, possess the right to do that. Palestine is an Islamic Waqf land consecrated for Muslim generations until Judgement Day. This being so, who could claim to have the right to represent Muslim generations till Judgement Day?

This is the law governing the land of Palestine in the Islamic Sharia (law) and the same goes for any land the Muslims have conquered by force, because during the times of (Islamic) conquests, the Muslims consecrated these lands to Muslim generations till the Day of Judgement." (The Covenant of the Islamic Resistance Movement, 18 August 1988, Article Three)

The Arab League Secretary General Azzam Pasha, said on 1 May 1948 thus even before the Jewish State was born:

"If the Zionists dare establish a state in Falastin, the massacre which will ensue here will dwarf anything which Genghis Khan and Hitler did."

Therefore, the acceptance of *Jihad* or 'holy war' comes easy to Islam. From its inception Islam has been a warring and very bloody, subjugating religion, which has not blushed at the use of war and terror but glorified it as the absolute will of Allah.

This then is the main problem. As long as Islam remains intolerant of really accepting any other group of people on an equal basis—rather than as dhimmies to be subjugated by Islam—there can never be a real peace with an Islamic power. Only a 'submission' (which is what Islam means) to its stated superiority and dictates. This awaits the whole world including the secular, often irreligious, West.

This is why the Muslim children chant, especially during the Middle East Wars: *"We shall fight on Saturday and then on Sunday."*

In other words, first the Jews and then the Christians. Make no mistake about this. When Israel will be swallowed up by the sea of Jihad, soon to be armed by weapons of mass destruction acquired by Muslim Iran and Muslim Iraq and others, the Muslims will believe that Allah has brought them to this point that they can finally reoccupy their Muslim Palestine and drive the Jews, the infidels as they would call them—into the sea as they have said and screamed many times in the name of their Allah.

We only need to look at the genocide by Muslims of over a million Christians in Southern Sudan, the massacres of Christians in Indonesia by Muslims and elsewhere not to mention the genocide of Armenian Christians in the past by Muslim Turks—to know that this chant is no empty threat.

But when Israel is no more their hands will be free to turn yet again to the West as they did in the sixth and seventh centuries when they were finally stopped in their Islamic invasion at Tours and Poitiers in the middle of France having conquered all areas of Europe from Istanbul to Vienna and from Morocco to the middle of France, including Spain. This time after Israel has been dealt with in true Islamic fashion they will try again.

Through their oil, wealth and the enormous spread of their religion through thousands of Mosques and millions of Muslim adherence all over the world, Islamic leaders believe the day has come to wipe out the humiliation of that defeat in Europe by the armies of Charles Martel and now re-conquer Europe and all the West for Allah thus adding also these territories Europe to become 'Dar al-Islam': part of the house and possession of Islam.

This however, is not seen or understood by the vast majority of the Western leaders, nor in that sense by most of the leaders of Israel. Therefore the West with all its diplomacy and myriads of trips to help find a solution to the Middle East conflict were unable to do so because of an unwillingness to face up to this central reason for the conflict. This essay tries to put the finger on this overall problem without which no solution will be found to this Middle East conflict.

Because of this its very nature from the beginning Mohammedans have believed that is their holy duty—to subject the whole world—even be it by force of Jihad - to the teaching of Islam.

The word '*Islam*' as has already been noted, expressed this very connotation: to submit. Therefore, there is little restraint if any with the fanatic adherents to this faith about using force, terrorism, war and cunning to attain this goal. Actually all of this is sanctified and rewarded by Allah.

As John Laffin writes in his book, *The Arab Mind*:

> *The fundamentalism and fanaticism of the Islamic revolution have affected Arab thinking and especially that of Shi'a Arabs ... as well as that of those Palestinians who are members or supporters of the PLO. They have embraced terrorism and violence as normal expressions of political opinion. (Page 169)*

Thus if the Jews or Israelis finally see one of their members snap and kill Muslims in an exasperation of fury—as Dr. Baruch Goldstein did in the Mosque at Hebron—practically the whole Israeli society blushes for three days, incrementing themselves for having allowed such an atrocious deed, apologising to the whole world.

There is hardly any such blush or incrimination on the Muslim side only maybe a faint apology mainly for political purposes towards the West that they, the Muslims, are against all acts of violence. But none of the self-incrimination seen at the Israeli and Western side for similar atrocities.

General Ariel Sharon, now Prime Minster, was not directly involved in the massacre of Muslim Arabs in Shatilla and Sabra in Lebanon by Phalangists. Nevertheless, Israel took to the streets in massive self incriminating demonstrations not against the Phalangists, the perpetrators of this cruel deed, but against their own leaders for not having foreseen it and thus allowing it to happen.

There is no such self-criticism even for acts and massacres much worse on the Muslim side. There the worst kind of terrorists are praised—not condemned—as being true and courageous martyrs for Allah who will be rewarded in heaven by beautiful damsels and wine.

This then is the difference we are dealing with and unless we are willing to confront it head on it will continue to dictate the gruesome realities of wars and violence still to come all in the name of Allah and Islam.

Take for instance the gruesome lynching and murder by Muslim Arabs in Ramallah seen on television sets worldwide. Was there any credible outcry of disgust by Arab or Muslim leaders at the sight of this heinous crime? No. For the built-in provision for violence and degradation of the non-Muslims or infidels in such a part of the philosophy and sadly practice of Islam that unless condemned in the strongest ways possible by those still courageous enough in the West it will not go away or cause ad true reversal of such practices in the Middle East.

Justice and Righteousness are indivisible. It counts for all. Listen to the rather courageous words of Zakariya Muhammad, a Palestinian intellectual:

> "I cannot understand the attitude of the Palestinian intellectuals toward the abominable murder of the two [Israeli] captive soldiers in Ramallah.... When I see a Palestinian intellectual sinking his teeth into the flesh of the Israeli intellectuals in his newspaper column without saying even one word of truth against the murders committed on our side - I sink into depression. Justice is one and cannot be divided. You cannot use the part that serves you and cast off the other part, because in so doing you destroy the very essence of justice, which is supposed to be the intellectual's principle weapon."

So what can we do if this all is such an integral part of the tenants of the Muslim faith if we want to reverse it and so have a chance to bring real peace to this trouble Middle East?

If it is true that the root problem of the Middle East conflict—or the Arab-Israeli conflict—to be found in the tenants of Islam then we have to address these tenants as the main reasons. Just as we in Europe would have had to address the tenets of Nazi ideology as being the main reasons and culprits for the terrible massacres and destruction all over Europe. We cannot say—as some indeed have done—that because people believe a certain ideology or even religion therefore we have to accept and respect this. This is probably the gravest error of our time. All in the name of this so-called tolerance the wicked or fanatics then triumph.

Now bringing it right up to the point because of which politicians so far failed to resolve this Israeli-Arab conflict—the burdensome stone or problem of Jerusalem 'claimed' by both religious Islam and Judaism as their 'holy' city and property. Islam hardly even recognizes any sanctity of this city or Temple Mount in relation to Judaism whereas the Jews bend over backwards to make room for the sensitivities and wishes of the Muslims, by allowing them to conduct their religious affairs on Judaism's most holy hill.

How would we go about solving—this seemingly insolvable problem—of Jerusalem? It is like the two mothers both claiming before King Solomon to be the true owners of the disputed baby. But one was lying. One of them was usurping her rights without any basis for she had stolen the baby—replacing it with her own dead baby. And that is exactly the story of Islam—they are the great usurpers - building their mosques preferably on sites formerly belonging to other faiths and then claiming it henceforth as belonging exclusively to themselves. This needs to be addressed as a lie and falsification of history—if we ever want to come to a righteous, true and just solution. One of the mothers was lying before the wise Solomon—it was not her baby.

Until this very day we see this endeavor to rewrite and alter history is perpetrated: MK Abdul Malik Dahamshe of the Democratic Arab Party stated the following on 24 March 1997:

That the Western Wall is holy to the Muslims is not new. We think, and also knowledgeable Israeli sources think, that the Western all is not associated with the remains of the Jewish Temple. When the Temple was destroyed not a single stone remained in place. The Western Wall is part of the Al-Aqsa Mosque complex. When Muhammad took his horse to Jerusalem - and it was a special horse - he tied it to the Western Wall before he ascended into heaven. Also, Jewish sources say that there is nothing connecting the Jews to the Western Wall.

Jerusalem is not, as is often held, the city of the three great monotheistic faiths. At the most it is the city of origin of two faiths: Judaism and Christianity.

Islam did not originate in Jerusalem, it originated in Mecca and Medina on the Saudi Arabian Peninsula. Not once is Jerusalem mentioned in the Koran, whereas the Bible mentions Jerusalem over 600 times. Therefore, Jerusalem is not in the same sense important to Islam, as it is holy to Judaism and Christianity.

The reason that Islam built the stunning golden Dome of the Rock on the Jewish Temple mount was to express its repudiation of Jewish or Christian claims of sanctity, thus usurping the right to call Jerusalem '*el-Quds*'—the holy city for Islam because Islam conquered it.

The interpretation of the Muslim legend that says that Mohammed on his nocturnal journey through Sinai, Bethlehem and Hebron arrived at the place of 'the Farther Mosque" when there was as yet no mosque on the Temple Mount—the time of that dream—was at a later date claimed by Muslims to have been the Mosque on the Temple Mount. Therefore today the Al-Aqsa Mosque carries that name: "The Farther mosque."

Here is how Eliyahu Tal describes this Muslim falsification of history:

> *Featured prominently in today's headlines, Al-Aqsa, at the time of Mohammed, was according to some Orientalists, an obscure mosque located in Arabia distanced from the Ka'aba the most venerated shrine in Mecca. It was a 'stopover' in the Prophet's nocturnal flight to Heaven as recounted in the Koran: "Glory be to him who transported his servant by night to Heaven from the Sacred Mosque to the Farther One." Al-Aqsa, in Arabic, means the farther, the extreme one (Ch. 17, Verse 1). Jerusalem, of course, is not mentioned at all, because at the time it was still under Byzantine rule.*

> *The Prophet, who died in CE 632 (six years before the city surrendered to the Muslims) could never have set foot in Jerusalem. The Arabic name of Jerusalem Al-Quds (The Holy One) is derived from "Beit-el-Muqadas" (e.g. 'Beit H'amikdash'), the Hebrew name for the Temple mount. The sanctity of Jerusalem was not enshrined in Islam at its inception, but was introduced into it after the death of Mohammed.*

Now if it is true as is here maintained that Islam's so called 'holy rights' to ownership of the Temple Mount and the Old City of Jerusalem: 'Al-Quds,' are mainly usurped rights - having replaced and driven out after their Islamic conquest the claims and sensitivities of other religions then they have not a just claim to this city in the way the Jews may have.

This is how I once expressed it in an article:

> *It is unbelievable how quickly the criticism has come, both from inside as well as outside of Israel, against Ariel Sharon, as if he is the one responsible for the wanton destruction and violence that has erupted all over the land of Israel, just because he as opposition leader wanted to visit the most holy place of Judaism on one of the high holy days of the Jews.*
>
> *How would British people react if their Buckingham Palace or the St. Paul's Cathedral had been taken over by invading Muslims who by building four Mosques around these places - as the Muslims have done on Israel's most holy and important place - would henceforth claim Buckingham Palace as their sole property being unwilling to even allow the British to visit their own historical royal residential site or bar them from even praying at St. Paul's Cathedral?*
>
> *Would there not be an outcry in Britain especially when on a British high holiday a leader of the Conservative opposition party would finally muster enough courage to visit one of these sites at a moment that a present Chamberlain-like British government would be willing to forfeit sovereignty over these two historic British places in order to placate the increasingly violent and dangerous Muslim population in England?*

Would also then the BBC scold the British Conservative leader for even daring to want to visit Buckingham Palace or St. Paul's, as they did Sharon?

Therefore how would the nations of the world react if the people of Israel would have invaded and conquered Saudi Arabia had built their most beautiful synagogue over the Ka'aba stone claiming henceforth sole and exclusive ownership over Mecca and the Muslim's most sacred shrine, demanding before the entire world what from henceforth is only a Jewish sacred place? The entire world would rebel.

This is exactly what the Muslims have done. Should this be rewarded as has been tried in Camp David and other venues of negotiations by pressurizing the Jewish people to give up their unique historic and divine right to Jerusalem and the biblical land of Israel for peace sake—a peace which according to the prophet Mohammed's example can be broken at will as soon as it would suit the Muslim powers?

After having signed the D.O.P. agreement in Oslo, Norway with Israeli leaders, Arafat said to an exclusive Muslim audience in a mosque in Johannesburg, South Africa, that he viewed this agreement he made as '*a despicable truce*' which he said he would be able to break as soon as it suited him—just as the prophet Mohammed broke his truce with the Kuraish Tribe in Saudi Arabia centuries ago.

So if this is true—and it is—what kind of truce or peace is Israel or the West expected to make with those who, even after the signing of such a peace agreement, can break it at will and then obliterate their opponent all in the name and for the sake of Islam and Allah?

Educating Women Could Change Everything

Izzeldin Abuelaish

An often overlooked aspect of Middle Eastern instability has been the subjugation of the region's female population. Educating and empowering women can eradicate some of the problems, according to Izzeldin Abuelaish, who serves as president and founder of Daughters for Life, an educational foundation for girls and women in the Middle East. Abuelaish believes that the oppression of women has resulted in men gaining almost exclusive power and making political decisions that have proven disastrous. In the following viewpoint, Abuelaish contends that more women having control in government would lead to policies resulting in far less violence.

L asting peace in the Middle East depends on empowering young women through education. By oppressing our young people and women, we don't have a new generation that is full of ideas and full of change.

According to a recent report by the Brookings Institute's Center for Universal Education, there are now 3.1m fewer children out of school in the Arab region than there were in 2002, but 8.5 million children still remain excluded. Many are poor girls living in areas of conflict and rural areas.

The report also says there is a mixed or "boomerang" dynamic for girls in the Middle East. Although girls are less likely to start school than boys, when they get there, they are more likely to

"The peace dividend of educating women in the Middle East," by Izzeldin Abuelaish, The Conversation, March 18, 2014. https://theconversation.com/the-peace-dividend-of-educating-women-in-the-middle-east-24453. Licensed under CC BY-ND 4.0.

make the transition from primary to secondary education – 97% make the transition compared to 91% of boys. They also tend to outperform boys in terms of learning.

But there is an urgent need to resume the disturbed balance in the relationship between men and women in the Middle East. At the moment, the future remains largely shaped by men. We need to see more women at the negotiation table, involved in politics and civil society. In Egypt and Syria, few women are talking. If women were a more vocal part of Syrian civil society, I'm sure the country would find another alternative than violence.

There are some very influential women leaders already in the Middle East. In the Palestinian authority, Dr Hanan Ashrawi served as the official spokesperson for the Palestinian delegation in the Middle East peace process, and is now a member of the executive of the Palestine Liberation Organisation. In February, she called for an law banning honour killings in the Middle East. But instead of having one Hanan, we need thousands.

Politics, culture, and men's power over girls and women in many developing countries are the major factors holding back women's education. To effect change we must develop tools to support women's educational aspirations. Education systems must also combat the influence of messages received through parents, peers, media and society in general.

A friend of mine's daughter is currently studying business at the American University at Sharjah in the United Arab Emirates. I asked my friend, will she then continue on to do a masters? "No", her mother said. "I want her to marry." My friend has a PhD; but her priority for her daughter is stability as a housewife, not a career as a business woman. Priorities in Arab countries still remain stiffly focused around marriage, reproduction and building a family.

It's time to fix the imbalance. Social injustice through denying girls and women the right opportunities and education adversely affects the status, relationship, stability, and health of individuals and communities.

We need to build education systems that help women and children to develop the skills and competencies to be active members in the community.

We need to work together to prevent wars and conflict in their infancy. Peace is the ultimate prize and women's education is the key to make this happen.

Is a World Government Viable?

Mark Beeson

The following viewpoint explores the vast differences between realism and idealism in the future of international politics, Here, Mark Beeson, who serves as a professor of international politics at the University of Western Australia, studies the viability of one world government, which many believe would solve problems in the Middle East by bringing all nations under one set of laws and ending territorial disputes. Beeson points out that attempts at creating a utopian society can be encouraged, but it would be difficult to end the religious and philosophical conflicts in the Middle East simply by eliminating national borders.

To say the idea of world government gets mixed reviews would be an understatement, to put it mildly. Many people dismiss the idea out of hand as either a utopian fantasy or a recipe for dictatorship by unaccountable elites bent on world domination.

Even those who don't lie awake at night fretting about black helicopters and what goes on in smoke-filled rooms packed with powerful vested interests quite justifiably worry about democratic accountability.

At an historical moment when democratic institutions around the world are suffering a crisis of legitimacy and being undermined by a rising tide of populism and xenophobia, making the case for world government is consequently getting increasingly difficult.

"On the difficulty of being a world citizen," by Mark Beeson, The Conversation, October 27, 2016. https://theconversation.com/on-the-difficulty-of-being-a-world-citizen-67660. Licensed under CC BY-ND 4.0.

The most promising example of institutionalised international cooperation we have yet seen—the European Union—is in crisis and has become synonymous with dysfunction. Britain's ill-advised decision to leave only reinforces the idea that such projects are definitively off the historical agenda.

Paradoxically enough, however, some of the smartest people on the planet continue to argue that not only is world government desirable, it's actually a functional necessity and one that will inevitably be realised. The only question is when.

The casual observer can be forgiven for feeling somewhat confused. Even those of us who take a professional interest in such matters can succumb to bouts of acute cognitive dissonance as we try to get our heads around what we—in this case the human race—need to do to survive in a civilised fashion.

The reality is that some problems such as climate change simply cannot be addressed by isolated "communities of fate" of a sort that have come to dominate politics and governance over the last four or five hundred years.

The fact that we all live within nationally demarcated boundaries is one of the defining features of modern political life. And it determines the existential variety, too. Those born in Victorian Britain thought they had won life's lottery—or those in the upper classes did, at least.

Even now, people are willing to risk their lives to get into "the West" with its implicit promise of affluence, peace and social stability. It's not hard to see why.

Some would say it was ever thus: throughout history, life has always been tough and uncertain for many—perhaps most—of the human race. Indeed, it's possible to make a plausible argument that we humans have collectively never had it so good.

But this rather abstract way of thinking about the human condition is not much consolation to those living in Syria rather than Sydney. For those of us fortunate enough in such privileged enclaves of peace and prosperity the question is whether we have obligations beyond borders.

Are we obliged to care about the fates of strangers we will never meet and whose lives only appear fleetingly, if at all, on our television screens?

At one level, the answer is clearly "no." Unless you subscribe to some sort of religious belief that obliges you to take an interest in the welfare of your fellow man or woman, no one can compel us to care. True, seeing children getting blown up night after night gets a bit wearing, but you can always literally and metaphorically switch off.

But even if we take this quite understandable approach to problems we can do little to address, they will not disappear from the world's political agenda or even from our consciousness. The fact is that we are stuck with them.

The world really is much more interconnected, interdependent and interactive than it has ever been before. What happens in one part of the world really can exert an influence elsewhere—even if it's only in an increasingly futile effort to seal off one part of the world from the problems of another.

It is precisely because of the global nature of many problems that some people think that world government, or at least an increasingly effective process of global governance, has to be part of the way we conduct human affairs, however unlikely that might seem in principle.

It is also becoming ever more apparent that even relatively humdrum policy issues such as taxation are becoming impossible to manage without high levels of international cooperation that transcend national boundaries.

Yet even if we accept that transnational cooperation is a necessity for achieving effective governance in everything from climate change, disaster relief, to the governance of myriad areas of economic and social life, actually doing this effectively and uncontroversially is much easier said than done.

Not only will some actors inevitably benefit more than others from such initiatives, but some states also remain implacably opposed to the very idea of anything that impinges on national sovereignty.

In East Asia where I do most of my research, states have a long history of jealously protecting national sovereignty and little enthusiasm for the sort of cooperation that characterised the European Union in its heyday.

Indeed, many in Asia feel vindicated by what has happened to the EU of late and read it as a cautionary tale of elite level hubris, rather than the most important attempt yet to transcend narrow national interests in pursuit of a more cosmopolitan common cause.

For students of international politics like me this is a real problem at both an intellectual and personal level. Part of me thinks that the arguments for greater international cooperation in the face of global problems are simply overwhelming and self-evident.

But I am also very familiar with Asia's empirical and historical record; it has created entrenched ideational and institutional obstacles to greater cooperation that are unlikely to be overcome in my lifetime—which is understandably the principal focus of my attention.

So what should those of us who would like to see greater collaboration occur actually do in the face of such seemingly insurmountable institutionalised obstacles? One response might be to follow Antonio Gramsci who said that he was "a pessimist because of intelligence, but an optimist because of will."

Developing forms of global citizenship, world government and a common consciousness do seem inherently improbable at this historical juncture. Believing in the possibility of change is vital, however, if only for our own psychological well being.

A World Government is a Good Idea—but Not Yet

Robin Hanson

In the following viewpoint, Robin Hanson, associate professor of economics at George Mason University, and research associate at the Future of Humanity Institute of Oxford University, rejects the idea of a world government becoming a reality via natural political evolution. Hanson believes that the threat of violence could achieve the same goal. He states that one possibility is the United Nations gaining control of all the militaries of the world—which would, in turn, make individual nations powerless. Hanson expresses a desire for an eventual world government, but feels that only a military monopoly can make that happen.

Several sources lately incline me to think of world (or solar) government as very likely in the long run. First, I read Bertrand Russell, in a 1950 essay *The Future of Mankind*, advocating violence to make a world government:

> *Before the end of the present century, unless something quite unforeseeable occurs, one of three possibilities will have been realized. These three are:*
> *I. The end of human life, perhaps of all life on our planet.*
> *II. A reversion to barbarism after a catastrophic diminution of the population of the globe.*

"Is World Government Inevitable?," by Robin Hanson, July 31, 2012 http://www.overcomingbias.com/2012/07/is-world-government-inevitable.html. Reprinted by Permission.

III. A unification of the world under a single government, possessing a monopoly of all the major weapons of war. ...

A world government is desirable. More than half of the American nation, according to a Gallup poll, hold this opinion. But most of its advocates think of it as something to be established by friendly negotiation, and shrink from any suggestion of the use of force. In this I think they are mistaken. I am sure that force, or the threat of force, will be necessary.

...

The governments of the English-speaking nations should then offer to all other nations the option of entering into a firm alliance, involving a pooling of military resources and mutual defense against aggression. In the case of hesitant nations, ... great inducements, economic and military, should be held out to produce their cooperation. ... When the Alliance had acquired sufficient strength, any Great Power still refusing to join should be threatened with outlawry, and, if recalcitrant, should be regarded as a public enemy. The resulting war ...

Russell was right that Americans then favored a world government:

In March 1951, nearly half (49%) of Americans thought the United Nations should be strengthened to make it a world government with power to control the armed forces of all nations, including the United States, while 36% thought it should not.

Seems they still favored it in 1993:

In a [1993] telephonic survey financed by the WFA, 58% of 1200 adult American citizens polled thought that to have practical law enforcement at home and abroad, a limited, democratic world government would be essential or helpful (with 35%) disagreeing). For effective enforcement of laws, 66% of those questioned felt there should be a world constitution, more than double the number who disagreed. ... 82% of respondents felt the UN Charter should be amended to allow the UN to arrest individuals who commit serious international crimes, and 83% felt that leaders making war on groups within their country should be tried by an International Criminal Court.

In 2007, much of the world also agreed:

A total of 21,890 people were interviewed between July 2006 and March 2007 [in 19 nations: US, Mexico, Argentina, Peru, Armenia, Ukraine, Russia, Poland, France, Pales. Terr., Israel, Australia, S. Korea, Thailand, China, Indonesia, India, Philippines, Iran.] ...

- *Large majorities approve of strengthening the United Nations by giving it the power to have its own standing peacekeeping force, regulate the international arms trade and investigate human rights abuses.*
- *Most publics believe the UN Security Council should have the right to authorize military force to address a range of problems, including aggression, terrorism, and genocide.*

Finally, the history of China suggests that, once started, "world" government becomes hard to stop:

This study explores the ways in which the Chinese imperial system attained its unparalleled endurance. ... I do not pretend to provide a comprehensive answer. ... Rather, I shall focus on a single variable, which distinguishes Chinese imperial experience from that of other comparable polities elsewhere, namely, the empire's exceptional ideological prowess. As I hope to demonstrate, the Chinese empire was an extraordinarily powerful ideological construct, the appeal of which to a variety of political actors enabled its survival even during periods of severe military, economic, and administrative malfunctioning. ...

Centuries of internal turmoil that preceded the imperial unification of 221 BCE ... were also the most vibrant period in China's intellectual history. Bewildered by the exacerbating crisis, thinkers of that age sought ways to restore peace and stability. Their practical recommendations varied tremendously; but amid this immense variety there were some points of consensus. Most importantly, thinkers of distinct ideological inclinations unanimously accepted political unification of the entire known civilized world—"All-under-Heaven"—as the only feasible means to put an end to perennial war; and they also agreed that the entire subcelestial realm should be governed by a single omnipotent monarch. These premises of unity and monarchism became the ideological foundation of the future empire, and they were not questioned for millennia.

Even if a world (or solar) government is inevitable, it is still probably best to not start it too early, before we are able to coordinate sufficiently well.

Chronology

1947

November 29   The United Nations General Assembly votes to separate Palestine into Jewish and Arab territories.

November 30   Conflict begins between Jewish and Arab groups in Palestine.

1948

May 14   Zionist leader David Ben-Gurion declares the independence of the state of Israel in part of Palestine partitioned to the Jews.

May 15   The armies of Syria, Egypt, Lebanon, and Jordan invade Palestine.

1949

January 7   A cease-fire ends the first Arab-Israeli War.

1964

May 29   The Palestine Liberation Organization is founded in Jerusalem.

1967

June 5-10   Israel defeats Arab armies in Six Day War; occupies West Bank, Gaza, East Jerusalem, Golan Heights, and Sinai Peninsula.

1972

September 5   Palestinian terrorist group Black September murders hostages from the Israeli Olympic team during the Munich Games.

1973

October 6-26   The Yom Kippur War allows Israel to seize more territory and ends in defeat for Syria.

1979

January 16   After the Shah is overthrown in Iran, that country's revolution begins.

March 26   Israel and Egypt sign Camp David Accords at the White House.

November 4   Sixty-three Americans are taken hostage by Iranian students.

December 24   The Soviet Union invades Afghanistan, launching a decade-long conflict.

1980

September 22   Iraq invades Iran; the war costs a half-million lives.

1981

October 6   Egyptian leader Anwar Sadat is assassinated by Islamic fundamentalists in Cairo.

1982

September 16   Hundreds of Palestinians are massacred in the Sabra and Shatila refugee camps outside Beirut.

1990

August 2 Iraq invades Kuwait.

1991

**January 16-
February 28** United States leads successful international effort to drive Iraq from Kuwait in the Persian Gulf War.

1996

January 21 Yasser Arafat is elected president of the Palestinian Authority.

May 29 Benjamin Netanyahu is elected prime minister in Israel.

2001

September 11 Terrorists attack New York and Washington with planes flown into the World Trade Center and the Pentagon.

2002

March 29 Israel invades Palestinian territories, reoccupies Palestinian cities.

2003

March 20 Iraq War begins as Americans invade.

2015

Sept. 13 More than 100 are killed by ISIS during attacks in Paris.

October The Iran nuclear deal is formally adopted.

Bibliography

Books

Ben Anderson. *No Worse Enemy: The Inside Story of the Chaotic Struggle for Afghanistan*. London, England: Oneworld Publications, 2013.

Scott Anderson. *Lawrence in Arabia: Deceit, Imperial Folly and the Making of the Modern Middle East*. New York: Anchor Books, 2014.

Jeremy Bernstein, *Nuclear Iran*. Cambridge, MA: Harvard University Press, 2014.

Mark Ensalaco. *Middle Eastern Terrorism: From Black September to September 11*. Philadelphia, PA: University of Pennsylvania Press, 2010.

John L. Esposito. *The Future of Islam*. Oxford, England: Oxford University Press, 2013.

Daniel Gordis. *Israel: A Concise History of a Nation Reborn*. New York: Ecco Press, 2016.

Nikki R. Keddie. Women in the Middle East: Past and Present. Oren, Michael B. *Six Days of War: June 1967 and the Making of the Modern Middle East*. New York: Presidio Press, 2003.

Nocola Pratt and Nadje Al-Ali. *Women and War in the Middle East: Transnational Perspectives*. London, England: Zed Books, 2008.

Abraham Rabinovich. *The Yom Kippur War: The Epic Encounter That Transformed the Middle East*. New York: Schocken Books, 2005.

Ali Soufan. *Anatomy of Terror: From the Death of Bin Laden to the Rise of the Islamic State*. New York: W.W. Norton, 2017.

Leslie Stein. *The Making of Modern Israel: 1948-1967.* Boston, MA: Polity, 2011.

Mark Tessler. *A History of the Israeli-Palestinian Conflict.* Bloomington, IN: Indiana University Press, 2009.

Joby Warrick. *Black Flags: The Rise of ISIS.* New York: Anchor Books, 2016.

Bob Woodward. *Plan of Attack: The Definitive Account of the Decision to Invade Iraq.* New York: Simon and Schuster, 2004.

Periodicals

Hussain Abdul-Hussain. "Peace Will Never Come to the Middle East." The Huffington Post. Accessed July 6, 2017. http://www.huffingtonpost.com/hussain-abdulhussain/peace-will-never-come-to_b_639393.html

Jessica Brandt and Robert L. McKenzie. "Addressing the Syrian Refugee Crisis." Brookings. December 16, 2016. Accessed May 5, 2017. https://www.brookings.edu/research/addressing-the-syrian-refugee-crisis-recommendations-for-the-next-administration/

Joel Beinin and Lisa Hajjar. "Primer on Palestine, Israel and the Arab-Israeli Conflict." Middle East Research and Information Project. 2014. Accessed July 6, 2017. http://www.merip.org/primer-palestine-israel-arab-israeli-conflict-new

Anand Gopal. "The Hell After ISIS." *The Atlantic.* May 2016. Accessed May 5, 2017. https://www.theatlantic.com/magazine/archive/2016/05/the-hell-after-isis/476391/

Michael R. Gordon. "On the Mosul Front, a Brutal Battle Against ISIS and Time." *New York Times.* April 26, 2017. Accessed May 5, 2017. https://www.nytimes.com/2017/04/26/world/middleeast/mosul-iraq-isis.

html?rref=collection%2Ftimestopic%2FIslamic%20
State%20in%20Iraq%20and%20 Syria%2Index0
(ISIS)&action=click&contentCollection=timestopics&
region=stream&module=stream_
unit&version=latest&contentPlacement=9&pgtype=collection

Tasnim Nazeer. "How Empowered Women in the Middle East
Can Spur Positive Change." Middle East Eye. March 8,
2015. Accessed May 5, 2017. http://www.middleeasteye.net/
columns/how-empowered-women-middle-east-can-spur-
positive-change-1736047910

Eyder Peralta. "6 Things You Should Know About the Iran
Nuclear Deal." National Public Radio. July 14, 2015.
Accessed May 5, 2017. http://www.npr.org/sections/thetwo-
way/2015/07/14/422920192/6-things-you-should-know-
about-the-iran-nuclear-deal

Cristina Silva. "Trump on Iraq War: U.S. 'Should Never Ever
Have Left.'" *Newsweek*. March 21, 2017. Accessed May
5, 2017. http://www.newsweek.com/trump-iraq-war-us-
should-never-ever-have-left-571524

Nick Thompson. "Syria's War: Everything You Need to Know
About How We Got Here." CNN. February 25, 2016.
Accessed May 5, 2017. http://www.cnn.com/2015/10/08/
middleeast/syria-war-how-we-got-here/

Index